INSTRUCTOR'S MANUAL AND TEST BANK
FOR

Social Gerontology
A MULTIDISCIPLINARY PERSPECTIVE
FOURTH EDITION

NANCY HOOYMAN
SCHOOL OF SOCIAL WORK
UNIVERSITY OF WASHINGTON

H. ASUMAN KIYAK
INSTITUTE ON AGING
UNIVERSITY OF WASHINGTON

Allyn and Bacon
Boston · London · Toronto · Sydney · Tokyo · Singapore

INSTRUCTORS MANUAL
TABLE OF CONTENTS

To The Instructor:

This "Instructor's Manual" is intended to assist you in designing your lesson plans and lectures for topics covered in the fourth edition of our textbook "Social Gerontology: A Multidisciplinary Perspective." A listing of key terms and concepts has been developed for each chapter. Some of these terms and concepts are repeated in different chapters. This allows each chapter to be used independently, without assuming that previous chapters have been assigned. In addition, several discussion topics have been included for each chapter to aid you in generating class discussion and essay questions for examinations. A series of multiple choice and true/false questions are also included for each chapter. These questions focus on the key concepts presented in the book. You will also find a Resource Directory of organizations, periodicals, and newsletters in the field of gerontology at the end of this manual. We hope you will find the "Instructor's Manual" to be a useful adjunct to the textbook and in teaching social gerontology.

NRH
HAK

INTRODUCTION: WHY STUDY AGING?

Key Terms

Geriatrics
Gerontology
Social gerontology
Types of aging
    Chronological
    Biological
    Psychological
    Social
  Ageism

Senescence
Cohort
Social environmental perspective
Person-environment transaction
Environmental press
Competence
Environmental intervention
Adaptive capacity
Age-graded

Topics for Discussion

1. Distinguish between different types of aging. To what extent would one expect consistency among these types of aging?

2. In what ways do societal structures and policies affect the study of social gerontology and the social well-being of the older population?

3. What historical and cultural factors have differentially influenced the cohort of people who are currently aged 65 to 75 and those aged 35 to 45?

4. Distinguish among the young-old, the old-old, and the oldest-old in terms of social and health characteristics.

5. Discuss the benefits of studying social gerontology from a dynamic person-environment transactional perspective.

Multiple Choice

1. Gerontology is the field of study that examines diverse aspects of aging. Geriatrics, on the other hand, focuses on:

   a. early childhood development
   b. maturation
X c. clinical aspects of aging
   d. economic well-being in old age

2. Changes that occur in sensory function, cognitive functioning and personality are a reflection of:

   a. chronological age
   b. biological aging
X c. psychological aging
   d. social aging

3. Which of the following topics are social gerontologists least likely to study?:

X a. biological aspects of aging
   b. economics of aging
   c. family structures
   d. housing for the older people

4. Changes in the organism throughout the life span occur in sequence. This sequence consists of the following steps:

   a. development and maturation
X b. development or maturation, senescence
   c. birth and maturation
   d. aging and development

5. Demands that the social and physical environment place on the individual are known as:

   a. environmental congruence
X b. environmental press
   c. transactions
   d. dynamic interactions

6. The theoretical upper limit of an indivdual's ability to function in health, cognition and behavior is known as:

X   a. individual competence
      b. social press
      c. individual adaptability
      d. maturation

7. Learning about the aging process can aid people in:

      a. adapting to their own aging
      b. reducing fears about aging
      c. understanding the aging of friends and family
X   d. all of the above
      e. none of the above

8. It is difficult to generalize about the older population because:

      a. aging cannot be defined only chronologically
      b. the older population is tremendously diverse
      c. there can be a range of 30 years between the young-old and the oldest-old
X   d. all of the above
      e. none of the above

True or False

1. In general, the chronological age of most people is consistent with their psychological and biological age.

    True__ False_X_

2. The cohort of young-old people today has lived through the Great Depression.

    True_X_ False__

3. Relocation to an unfamiliar environment is an example of increased environmental press in Lawton and Nahemow's model.

    True_X_ False__

4. Older people who are experiencing declines in competence would benefit from a move to a nursing home.

    True__ False_X_

5. Early research in the field of gerontology tended to be theoretical rather than applied.

    True_X_ False__

6. The study of aging is primarily a study of diseases.

    True__ False_X_

CHAPTER 1: GROWTH OF THE OLDER POPULATION

Key Terms

Life expectancy
Maximum life span
Survival curves
Population pyramids
Dependency ratios
Elderly support ratio
Compression of morbidity

Ethnic minorities
Crossover effect
Active vs. dependent life expectancy
Attitudes
The new ageism
Age discrimination
Compassionate stereotypes

Topics for Discussion

1. Discuss the influence of mortality and birthrates, as well as life expectancy, on the significant increase observed in the older population today.

2. Discuss some factors that affect differential life expectancy for men vs. women.

3. What are the economic, political, and social implications of the increasing rectangularization of the population pyramid?

4. Discuss the implications of the growth of the oldest-old for social and health services in the U.S.

5. Discuss the pros and cons of using dependency ratios as a predictor of the potential burden of a particular age group on society.

6. Discuss the age distribution among ethnic minority groups today and patterns that are emerging for the future.

7. Describe the phenomenon of the crossover effect and implications for working with older minority men and women.

8. Discuss the geographic distribution of the older U.S. population and implications for policies in states with higher and lower than average proportions of older persons in their population.

9. What are some reasons for the growth of the older population in developing countries?

10. Describe some alternatives to the hypothesis of compressed morbidity for future cohorts of elderly persons.

11. Design a training program for health professionals (nurses, physicians, social workers, dentists) that will reduce stereotypes toward the elderly and result in more realistic views of this population.

Multiple Choice

1. Over the past ten years, increases in life expectancy after age 65 have:

   X   a. been relatively modest
        b. declined
        c. increased, more for women than for men
        d. increased, more for men than for women

2. The greatest growth in the U.S. population since 1960 has been among the:

        a. baby boomers
        b. young-old
        c. old-old
   X   d. oldest-old

3. As societies become more advanced with improvements in health care and sanitation, the survival curve becomes:

        a. flatter
   X   b. more rectangular
        c. steeper
        d. bimodal

4. Population pyramids for the U.S. will become:

   X   a. more rectangular
        b. more pyramid-like
        c. difficult to project
        d. elongated

5. It is a fallacy to assume that the changing elderly dependency ratios will result in increased burdens on younger people because:

        a. more people are working into advanced old age
        b. the dependency ratio has not changed since 1910
        c. fewer women are entering the labor force
   X   d. those under age 16 are the largest "dependent" group

6. Compared to their white counterparts, the proportion of African American men to women is higher among the :

        a. baby boomers
        b. young old
        c. old-old
   X   d. oldest-old

7. The population groups in the U.S. with the smallest proportion of people 65+ are:

     a. Whites and Hispanics
     b. African Americans and Whites
X   c. Hispanics and American Indians
     d. Pacific Asians and African Americans

8. Differences between whites and African Americans in life expectancy at age 65 are:

     a. greater than differences in life expectancy at birth
X   b. less than differences in life expectancy at birth
     c. about the same as life expectancy at birth
     d. due to higher infant mortality among whites

9. The state with the highest median age today is _____; that with the lowest is _____.

     a. Florida/Alaska
X   b. Florida/Utah
     c. Arkansas/South Dakota
     d. Iowa/Rhode Island

10. Compared to the United States, the ratio of workers to retirees in Japan and Europe is becoming _____.

     a. more pyramid-like
     b. less rectangular
     c. greater
X   d. smaller

11. The growing discrepancy between the poor and non-poor in the U.S. is expected to lead to:

     a. class wars
     b. more need for hospitals for older persons
X   c. a bimodal distribution of healthy and frail elders
     d. more women remaining healthy, more men dying younger

12. The distinction between active and dependent life expectancy is useful in illustrating:

     a. differences between men and women
X   b. that not all gains in life expectancy are positive
     c. that most of the gain in life expectancy is a negative gain
     d. the advantages of increased life expectancy for ethnic minorities

13. Federal policies that place demands on families to care for their elderly are based on:

    a. ageist attitudes
    b. beliefs in individual rights
X   c. historical stereotypes about family roles
    d. idealized stereotypes about family roles in other countries

14. Social contact can reduce the likelihood of stereotyping if the following conditions exist:

    a. daily contact with nursing home elderly
    b. the two groups establish role distinctions
X   c. an atmosphere of egalitarianism is created
    d. the groups exchange social roles

15. Which of the following is not true of stereotypes?

    a. They are generalized beliefs about a group
X   b. They are always negative
    c. They often are unrealistic
    d. They simplify our perception of the world around us

16. It has been argued and supported by research that "Compassionate stereotypes" about the older population in the U.S. have resulted in:

    a. reductions in public support for elders
X   b. more public programs to help elders
    c. resentment by the young against the old
    d. increased interest in gerontology as a career

17. All of the following may give rise to negative attitudes about the elderly except:

X   a. extensive contact with diverse elderly
    b. anxieties about one's own aging
    c. fear of the unknown
    d. competition for scarce resources

18. Intergenerational living arrangements that reduce stereotypes have the following feature:

    a. young family members take care of their elders
    b. grandparents support the grandchildren financially
    c. grandparents are physically healthy
X   d. the relationship is mutually interdependent

True or False

1. Life expectancy refers to the average years of life one can expect to live, whereas maximum life span refers to the maximum number of years a given species is expected to live.

   True _X_ False __

2. In 1985 the U.S. had proportionately more people over age 65 in its population than did any other industrial country.

   True __ False _X_

3. The maximum lifespan has increased significantly since 1900.

   True __ False _X_

4. Today, life expectancy among older minorities is very similar to that of whites.

   True __ False _X_

5. The proportion of people aged 65 and older among ethnic minority groups will remain essentially unchanged in the 21st century.

   True __ False _X_

6. Pacific Asian older men are more likely than any other ethnic group to live alone.

   True _X_ False __

7. Trends in the health status of middle-aged people today provide only moderate support for compressed morbidity in the future.

   True _X_ False __

8. The greatest proportion of elders live in rural areas.

   True __ False _X_

9. The high proportion of older adults in Florida is due to in-migration of elders, while that of South Dakota is due to out-migration of younger persons.

   True _X_ False __

10. By increasing one's social contact with an unknown group or its members, one usually develops more positive attitudes about them.

    True __ False _X_

11. Advertisers have been slower than TV and film producers to portray older persons in a realistic, positive manner.

   True _X_   False __

12. Ageism refers to the feelings of prejudice based on someone's age alone.

   True _X_   False __

13. Courses in gerontology usually lead to developing a compassionate stereotype of the older population and behaving in an egalitarian manner toward all older persons.

   True __   False _X_

14. As the media begins to portray more positive images of older persons, stereotypes about aging and the older population will be reduced.

   True _X_   False __

15. Many older persons have learned to cope with societal stereotypes of aging by denying their age and acting like teenagers.

   True __   False _X_

CHAPTER 2: THE OLDER POPULATION AND HOW IT IS STUDIED

Key Terms

Age-period-cohort problem
Age changes vs. age differences
Cross-sectional research
Longitudinal research
Sequential research designs
    Cohort-sequential
    Time-sequential
    Cross-sequential
Attrition
Selective dropout

Terminal drop
Social distance scales
Semantic differential technique
Social contact hypothesis
Discrimination
Components of attitudes
    Cognitions (beliefs)
    Evaluations (affect)
    Behavioral intentions
Attitude measurement

Topics for Discussion

1. To what extent has the field of social gerontology grown as a result of social policies, the aging of the population, and interest in this as an academic field? Give examples for each of these influences.

2. Compare your own experiences as members of a birth cohort with those from the cohorts of the 1920's and 1930's.

3. Describe the age/period/cohort problem in social gerontological research. What research designs have been developed to overcome some of these problems? What are the strengths and weaknesses of each design?

4. Discuss the advantages and disadvantages of conducting longitudinal research in aging.

5. Discuss some of the major longitudinal studies of aging and their contribution to our understanding of aging and older adults.

6. Describe examples of cross-sectional studies in which age <u>differences</u> have been erroneously inferred by the public as illustrating age <u>changes</u>.

7. Discuss the components of attitudes and provide some hypotheses on why these components may be inconsistent. To what extent is each component of attitudes predictive of behavior toward unfamiliar groups of people?

8. Discuss the strengths and weaknesses of existing measures of stereotypes toward aging and older adults.

Multiple Choice

1. The earliest research centers (pre-1960) established to study gerontology include all <u>except</u> the following:

       a. The Baltimore City Hospital
X   b. The National Institute on Aging
       c. The Duke University Center on Aging
       d. The University of Chicago Center on Aging

2. In order to understand age changes as distinct from age differences, it is necessary to conduct:

X   a. longitudinal research
       b. cross-sectional research
       c. cross-cultural research
       d. long-lasting studies of different ethnic groups

3 A major <u>advantage</u> of longitudinal research designs is that they:

       a. allow for practice effects
X   b. eliminate cohort effects
       c. allow a distinction between age and time by testing
       d. compare different groups

4. A research design that alleviates the problems of cross-sectional and longitudinal studies, and is useful for distinguishing between age and historical factors, is known as a:

       a. sequential design
X   b. time-sequential design
       c. cohort-sequential design
       d. cross-sequential design

5. A researcher wants to examine changing attitudes toward welfare among people of different cohorts. She conducts interviews with people born in 1930 and 1950 during 1985, and again in 1995. This is an example of a:

       a. longitudinal design
       b. cohort-sequential design
X   c. cross-sequential design
       d. time-sequential design

6. Which of the following types of research is the best method for comparing groups of people at one point in time?

X   a. cross-sectional
     b. longitudinal
     c. sequential
     d. none of the above

7. A valid measure is one that:

     a. yields the same result from repeated measurements
X   b. accurately reflects the concept it is intended to measure
     c. is used only in cross-sectional studies
     d. is used only in psychological testing

8. A researcher wants to determine the range of oral disease among the older population by examining the mouths of all 200 residents of a nursing home. The findings cannot be generalized to all older people because:

     a. the sample is not valid
     b. the data are not reliable
     c. the concept is not correctly measured
X   d. the sample is not representative

9. The problem of trying to reach ethnic minority elders from the membership list of AARP is that:

X   a. they are under-represented in this group
     b. only the sickest are likely to be members
     c. they are over-represented in this group
     d. they do not represent the geographic diversity of ethnic groups

10. Selective dropout from longitudinal studies results in:

     a. poorer test scores with time
X   b. healthier and more motivated elders in the final sample
     c. sicker and less educated elders in the final sample
     d. few differences between drop-outs and those who remain

11. Research among various adult populations has revealed that affect toward older persons is generally:

     a. very positive
     b. very negative
     c. between negative and neutral
X   d. between neutral and positive

12. Increased contact with an outgroup under appropriate conditions should result in:

    a. more positive attitudes toward the outgroup
X   b. more realistic attitudes toward the outgroup
    c. improved self-concept among participants
    d. increased liking of outgroup members

13. Measures of stereotypes toward older persons generally allow closed-ended true-false responses. These often have the danger of confounding stereotypes with:

    a. dislike of older people
    b. protectionism toward older people
X   c. misinformation about a given fact
    d. test-taking ability

14. Level of education has been found to be related to:

X   a. knowledge of older people
    b. affect toward older people
    c. acceptance of older people's infirmities
    d. the desire to work with older people

15. Semantic differential techniques generally have been used to assess:

    a. stereotypes
X   b. affect
    c. social distance
    d. acceptability of an outgroup

16. Behavior of younger people toward older persons can be <u>accurately</u> predicted by their:

    a. stereotypes about aging and older people
    b. affect toward older people in general
    c. educational level
    d. all of the above
X   e. none of the above

17. Ethical guidelines for conducting research with older persons:

X   a. have not been developed
    b. have been published by the National Institute on Aging
    c. have been proposed by the AARP
    d. discourage conducting research with cognitively impaired elders.

True or False

1. The earliest studies in gerontology were conducted in the nineteenth century and focused on physiological and biological aging.

    True _X_   False __

2. Cross-sectional research designs are the best method to determine causation.

    True __   False _X_

3. Older people who drop out of longitudinal studies tend to be those who score lower on intelligence tests and are more socially isolated.

    True _X_   False __

4. Longitudinal studies are currently the most widely used research designs in gerontology.

    True __   False _X_

5. Cross-sectional studies confound age and cohort effects.

    True _X_   False __

6. Cohort-sequential designs confound cohort effects and time of measurement.

    True _X_   False __

7. Time-sequential designs are useful in distinguishing between age and cohort.

    True __   False _X_

8. Sequential designs are particularly useful in studies of cognitive changes with aging.

    True _X_   False __

9. There is a strong association between negative attitudes toward a group and one's behavior toward members of that group.

    True __   False _X_

10. Studies in which young people have had increased contact with frail elders in nursing homes have not found increased affect toward all older persons.

    True _X_   False __

CHAPTER 3: HISTORICAL AND CROSS-CULTURAL ISSUES IN AGING

Key Terms

Comparative sociocultural gerontology
Gerontocide
Senecide
Modernization
Age equality
Veneration of elders
Filial piety

Sources of power
   property
   political
   knowledge
Reciprocity
Acceptance of dependency
Traditional/transitional societies

Topics for Discussion

1.   What has been the impact of modernization on the status and role of older people in different cultures?

2.   What specific aspects of modernization contribute to a change in older people's social status? In addition to modernization, what other reasons explain changes between generations in American society?

3.   What factors may influence the differential social status of older people in different societies at the same stage of modernization?

4.   To what extent can older people maintain power in a social system through control of knowledge and property? Describe any gender differences that may arise in this ability to control resources.

5.   It has been suggested that the study of aging in other cultures is of intrinsic interest but has no relevance to an understanding of old age in our own society. Argue the pros and cons of this proposition.

6.   Discuss the changing status and roles of older people from prehistoric through colonial times.

7.   What influence does the physical and cognitive status of an older person have on society's response toward older people?

8.   Discuss the role of economic changes in societies such as Japan and China filial piety and multigenerational households.

Multiple Choice

1. Old age in prehistoric times was characterized by:

   a. respect and a sense of sacred obligation toward elders
   b. gerontocide toward the very old and unhealthy
   c. few people living to an advanced old age
   d. gerontocide being carried out with great reverence
   X e. all of the above

2. In classical civilizations, the aged who benefited the most from respect to elders were:

   a. all men
   b. all older people
   X c. men from the elite classes
   d. mothers of the tribal leaders

3. The growth of democracy in fifth century Greece was generally associated with:

   a. increasing veneration of the aged
   X b. increasing exaltation of youth
   c. respect for older people's power
   d. respect for wisdom

4. Old age in Colonial America was characterized by:

   X a. veneration toward elders
   b. considerable affection or love for elders
   c. low status of elders
   d. frequent interaction between young and old

5. In the 19th and 20th centuries, demographic patterns shifted so that:

   X a. parents generally lived many more years after their children left home
   b. more older people assumed positions of prestige and power
   c. more older people were dependent on their children
   d. more multigenerational families lived together

6. According to modernization theory, the status of the older population has declined because of:

   a. health technology that has prolonged adult life
   b. scientific technology that has made traditional occupations held by the older persons obsolete
   c. efforts to promote literacy and education
   d. urbanization
   X e. all of the above

7. Among the important resources controlled by older people that enhance their positions in society, which is the least important one?

    a. knowledge of traditional skills
X   b. chronological age
    c. information control
    d. their social contributions

8. According to Fischer, the decline in older people's status is due to:

    a. industrialization and civilization
    b. the increase in the number of older people
X   c. our cultural values of liberty and equality
    d. modernization

9. The major premise of modernization theory is that:

    a. with modernization, the status of older people always increases
    b. with modernization, there are more opportunities for interaction between old and young
    c. with improved health technology, older people experience a higher quality of life
X   d. with modernization, older people often lose political and social power

10. As wealth became an increasing source of social identity in America, there was a shift in the 19th and 20th centuries toward:

    a. greater prestige accorded the older population
    b. declining intergenerational ties
    c. growing recognition of the need to support older family members
X   d. growing veneration of youth and contempt of old age

11. Which of the following statements about the care of older persons in Japan is true?

    a. Traditionally, Japanese families have cared for their members, and this pattern has not changed significantly.
    b. Japanese families assume no more responsibility for their older relatives than do Western families.
X   c. Traditionally, Japanese families have cared for their older relatives, but that pattern is eroding.
    d. The old are such a small proportion of the Japanese population that their care is not a significant problem.

12. Knowledge as a source of power for older people is often undermined in societies where:

X   a. scientific advances supersede traditional knowledge
    b. money assumes decreased value
    c. rituals become less formal
    d. educational institutions reject the contributions of older members

13. The traditional roles of elderly in Japan have changed as a result of all except the following:

    a. increased urbanization
    b. declining birthrate
    c. more women in the labor force
X   d. Western influence regarding age equity

14. A variety of factors can offset the societal costs of maintaining the older populations. These are older people's:

    a. contacts with powerful others
    b. ability to perform domestic tasks
    c. political power
    d. ritual power
X   e. all of the above

15. Which of the following is not a traditional source of power for the elderly in most societies?

    a. control of property
X   b. government benefits that accrue to older members
    c. filial piety within the extended family
    d. knowledge

16. Benign neglect of older people is generally accepted:

    a. in all modern societies
    b. in traditional societies
X   c. in some societies when the older person is physically or cognitively impaired
    d. in some societies when the older person provides no financial help to the family

True or False

1. Comparative sociocultural gerontology allows us to study the biological processes of aging.

     True___   False_X_

2. Old age was first defined in chronological terms (e.g., age 60 and over) in Greek and Roman cultures.

     True_X_   False___

3. The increase in median age that occurred in the early 19th century was due primarily to the declining death rate.

     True___   False_X_

4. In most societies, older people's status is largely determined by the balance between their perceived contributions to society and the cost of maintaining them.

     True_X_   False___

5. Shakespeare attributed wisdom and power to old age.

     True___   False_X_

6. Old age was viewed as a sign of God's favor by the Puritans.

     True_X_   False___

7. The Colonial era is marked by a time of close intergenerational bonds.

     True___   False_X_

8. According to modernization theory, old age becomes more venerated in society as the culture becomes more technologically developed.

     True___   False_X_

9. Filial piety was generally reserved for older people of higher social classes in traditional Chinese culture.

     True_X_   False___

10. In nineteenth century America, egalitarian values did not extend to economic equality; old age no longer was equated with economic power.

     True_X_   False___

11. Filial piety in traditional cultures can be significantly undermined in societies if resources become scarce.

   True _X_   False __

12. Older people have been able to retain their positions of prestige in most societies by continuing to be employed.

   True __   False _X_

13. In some religious groups, the most sacred rituals are reserved for the elders of that group.

   True _X_   False __

CHAPTER 4: SOCIAL THEORIES OF AGING

Key Terms

Propositions or hypotheses
Social theories
Role theory
    Age norms
    Role gain
    Role loss
    Role stability
    Role ambiguity
    Role discontinuity
Life-span perspective
Kansas City Studies of Adult life
Activity theory
Disengagement theory
Continuity theory
Theory of patterned differentiation of aging
Subculture of aging

Age stratification theory
Allocation of roles
Socialization to roles
Cohort flow
"Cohort-centric"
"Age-irrelevant" society
Symbolic interactionist perspective
Labeling theory
Social breakdown theory
Social reconstruction theory
Social exchange theory
Sources of power for older people
Political economy of aging

Topics for Discussion

1. List several ways that an older person may act that are contrary to age norms. What happens when an older individual violates age norms?

2. Debate the question: Do older people constitute a distinct subculture?

3. Which theory in this chapter is most consistent with your own view of aging? What evidence supports this theory?

4. Which theory described in this chapter could provide you with useful guidelines for working with older people in community based settings? Give examples of practice guidelines that you could derive from this particular theoretical perspective.

5. What common themes do you see in the ways that both older people and our social institutions attempt to deal with the issue of dependency?

6. According to Sharon Curtin in Nobody Ever Died of Old Age, "There is nothing to prepare you for the experience of growing old." Based upon the theoretical perspectives in this chapter, how would you advise younger adults to prepare for this experience? How will you approach your own aging?

7. What theories are reflected in current social policies toward older people? How can exchange theory be used to justify reductions in services and benefits for older people?

Multiple Choice

1. Social theories of aging address the basic question of:

X   a. the optimal way for older people to adapt
    b. how older people socialize
    c. older people's needs vis-a-vis family interactions
    d. the impact of physiological changes on older people

2. Which of the following is true concerning changes in roles that occur with age?

    a. Role losses are largely irreversible.
    b. Role losses can lead to a decline in self esteem.
    c. Role gains are impossible .
    d. all of the above.
X   e. a & b

3. Growing old may imply some new kinds of dependency. In working with older people,which one of the approaches listed below,would help him or her accept unavoidable dependency with dignity?

    a. Draw their attention to all the roles they have lost
X   b. Create a sense of giving and receiving in their relationships
    c. Help them deny their losses and act as if nothing has happened
    d. Remind them that all older people lose power as they age and that they aren't so bad off

4. A theory that is consistent with society's values of work and productivity is:

    a. cognitive-behavioral theory
X   b. activity theory
    c. continuity theory
    d. role theory

5. One of the major limitations of activity theory is:

    a. it fails to acknowledge the role of personality
    b. it assumes that older people want to maintain the standards of middle age
    c. it assumes that older people are able to continue the activities of middle age
    d. none of the above
X   e. all of the above.

6.   The life span perspective on aging:

a. views development as steady growth
b. focuses only on individual change
X   c. takes account of variation in functions over time
d. none of the above

7.   The theory that proposes that people seek more passive social roles as they age is called:

a. cognitive
b. activity
c. social reconstruction
X   d. disengagement

8.   A major limitation of activity theory and disengagement theory is that:

a. they both focus on healthy older people only
b. they both focus on the best way to age
X   c. neither addresses the historical or cultural context of aging
d. neither addresses the biological context of aging

9.   One of the shortcomings of disengagement theory is:

a. it assumes that older people identify only with one another
b. it assumes that people maintain typical ways of adjusting to the environment
   as they age
c. it assumes that older adults are discriminated against because of their age
X   d. it assumes that withdrawal from social roles is functional and experienced by
   most older people

10.   The theory based on the assumption that people have a basic core personality that remains
fairly stable throughout adulthood and old age is:

a. disengagement
X   b. continuity
c. exchange
d. role

11. A major contribution of the Kansas City Studies of Adult Life to the development of social theories of aging has been:

    a. recognition of how social structures affect older people's behavior
    b. attention to the variables of gender, race, and class
X   c. emphasis on the social psychological aspects of aging
    d. none of the above

12. A basic assumption of age stratification theory is:

    a. every society is stratified in terms of socioeconomic class.
    b. older persons form an age strata because of their age-based consciousness.
X   c. age is a universal criterion by which people's roles, rights, and privileges are distributed.
    d. the factors of life course dimension and historical dimension explain similarities in people's behaviors and attitudes.

13. Which theory states that people age most successfully by remaining involved in as many roles as possible and finding substitutes for lost roles?

    a. continuity
X   b. activity
    c. disengagement
    d. integrity

14. Constructs central to the theory of patterned differentiation of the aging process include all of the following except for:

    a. personality type, life satisfaction, and social integration
    b. four dominant life styles
X   c. a single successful lifestyle
    d. autonomy and persistence

15. The following is (are) true of age norms:

    a. they have no effect on the roles available to a person at any given age.
    b. they are biologically determined.
X   c. they determine societal expectations about what persons of a certain age should or should not do.
    d. all of the above

16.   The dynamic nature of age stratification is exemplified by:

     a. people getting on and off an escalator
     b. older people interacting only with their own peers
     c. the process of downward age mobility
X   d. the movement upward on an escalator to increasing age strata

17.   Which of the following social theories states that social intervention in the environment to improve older people's lives is desirable and possible?

     a. disengagement
X   b. social reconstruction
     c. age stratification
     d. subculture

18.   Which of the following assumptions are fundamental to the social exchange theory of aging?

     a. power or the control of valued resources
     b. Older adults have limited access to valued resources compared to younger people
     c. Dependence and deference characterize the interactions of many older people
     d. Most people try to maintain some reciprocity in their interactions
X   e. all of the above

19.   Which of the following types of changes refer to the events in society experienced by groups of people born at approximately the same time?

     a. age-graded
X   b. cohort
     c. unique
     d. none of the above

20.   The political economy perspective maintains that:

     a. on the basis of their shared experiences with discrimination, older people have developed a cohesive subculture.
     b. structural factors have defined older adults as a problem to be solved.
     c. older individuals tend to withdraw from the labor market, which is beneficial to the economy.
     d. fundamental policy changes are needed to alter both how older people are defined and their objective life conditions.
X   e. all of the above

True or False

1. Social theories of aging have been adequately tested so that we are able to predict with considerable accuracy the behavior of older individuals.

    True _____   False _X_

2. Scientific theories serve as a guide to further research.

    True _X_   False _____

3. Most empirical research on disengagement theory fails to support it.

    True _X_   False _____

4. In social exchange theory, when one person is dependent upon another, the latter achieves power.

    True _X_   False _____

5. According to the symbolic interactionist perspective, older individuals are discriminated against because of their age.

    True _____   False _X_

6. According to social exchange theory, older people disengage from society because it is beneficial both to themselves and to society.

    True _____   False _X_

7. According to disengagement theory, people age most successfully if they withdraw from active involvement in society.

    True _X_   False _____

8. One of the implications of the political economy perspective is the need to develop more medical services for older adults.

    True _____   False _X_

9.   The political economy perspective examines the larger sociopolitical conditions that underlie current policies and practices toward the older population.

     True _X_   False ____

10. Socialization into old age is easy for most people because of the widespread availability of positive role models.

     True ____   False _X_

CHAPTER 5: THE SOCIAL CONSEQUENCES OF BIOLOGICAL AGING

Key Terms

Biological theories
  Wear and tear theory
  Autoimmune theory
  Cross-linkage theory
  Free radical theory
  Cellular aging theory
Antioxidants
Collagen
Melanin
Senescence
Growth hormone

Hypothermia
Hyperthermia
Kyphosis
Reserve and vital capacity
Active life expectancy
Neuronal loss
Reaction time
Survival curve
Lipofuscin
Osteoporosis
Atherosclerosis
Lipofuscin

Topics for Discussion

1.	Several biological theories of aging have emerged over the past 20 years. Provide a critical analysis of each theory in terms of how it helps our understanding of the aging process, and its potential for reversing that process.

2.	Discuss some of the recent discoveries with human growth hormones and their effects of extending the life span and/or active life expectancy.

3.	In what ways could specific changes in body composition with aging influence an older person's reactions to medications and alcohol?

4.	Discuss some physiological and environmental risk factors for hypothermia in older people. What environmental interventions could be provided to alleviate these risks?

5.	Discuss the problem of hyperthermia in older people. What are the individual and environmental risk factors involved? How can it affect the older person's cognitive functions?

6.	Describe how people adapt to declines in several areas of physiological functioning with age.

7.	Compare normal, age-related changes in different organ systems. Which systems show the greatest change? Which the least? Suggest environmental interventions to alleviate the impact of some of these organ system changes on the older person.

Multiple Choice

1. Senescence refers to:

       a. senility in old age
    X b. the normal process of changes over time in the body
       c. abnormal changes that occur in the body with aging
       d. a type of gland in the body

2. Organ systems decline at differing rates among people. All of the following factors influence senescence except:

    X a. level of education
       b. heredity
       c. physical activity
       d. environmental toxins and stress

3. The biological theory that proposes that each species has a biological clock that determines its maximum life span and the rate at which each organ system will deteriorate is known as:

       a. disengagement
       b. the cross-linkage theory
    X c. the wear and tear theory
       d. the antioxidant theory

4. According to the free radical theory, the aging process may be slowed down with the ingestion of:

       a. Vitamin A
    X b. Vitamin E
       c. Vitamin C
       d. Lecithin

5. All of the following interventions have been shown to improve active life expectancy in lab animals except:

       a. vitamin E
       b. growth hormones
    X c. increasing hours of sleep
       d. caloric restriction

6.   All of the following changes occur in body composition with advancing age <u>except</u>:

     a. an increase in the proportion of fat
     b. an increase in fibrous material
     c. an increase in the sodium/potassium ratio
X   d. an increase in the proportion of water

7.   Reduced elasticity of connective tissue in the skin takes place with aging in:

     a. the epidermis
X   b. the dermis
     c. melanin
     d. subcutaneous skin

8.   Changes in the temperature regulatory system with aging result in a preference by older persons for ambient temperatures that are:

     a. much warmer than for younger people
     b. much cooler than for younger people
     c. a few degrees cooler than for younger people
X   d. a few degrees warmer than for younger people

9.   Maximum body size and strength generally reach their peak at age:

     a.   15
X   b.   25
     c.   35
     d.   45

10. Kyphosis is a condition in which:

     a.   physical strength declines
     b.   hair follicles deteriorate rapidly
X   c.   crush fractures occur in the spine
     d.   there is a shortage of vitamin D

11. Respiratory function in aging:

     a.   declines at a similar rate among all people
X   b.   declines more slowly among physically active people
     c.   is impaired primarily because of environmental pollutants
     d.   is equally impaired in smokers and non-smokers

12. Physical training among sedentary older persons has been shown to result in:

      a. increased death rates
      b. significant reductions in cholesterol levels
      c. reduced vital capacity
X   d. significant increases in aerobic capacity

13. Physical activity by older persons can increase their:

X   a. active life expectancy
      b. expected life span
      c. feelings of depression
      d. blood pressure

14. Among all organ systems, the one that has been found to decline most in structure and function with normal aging is:

      a. the respiratory system
      b. the heart
X   c. the kidneys
      d. the central nervous system

15. Urinary incontinence among older people generally is _not_ due to:

      a. a decline in the capacity of the bladder
      b. diseases associated with the nervous system
      c. changes in the brain that affect the sensation to void
X   d. increased consumption of tea and coffee

16. All of the following may influence the increased incidence of constipation in older persons except:

X   a. eating high fat foods
      b. lack of exercise
      c. structural changes in the large intestine
      d. decreased muscle tone in colon

17. Slower reaction time with aging is most likely due to:

X   a. slower response of neurotransmitters
      b. a rapid accumulation of lipofuscin in the brain
      c. a loss of brain mass
      d. anxiety about test taking

18.   Research on sleep patterns with normal aging reveal that older people:

       a.   sleep longer than young persons
       b.   spend more time in sleep stages 1,2,3
X   c.   spend less time in sleep stages 3,4,5
       d.   sleep more soundly than young persons

True or False

1. Aging may be attributable to the finite number of cell replications as the organism ages chronologically, according to one biological theory of aging.

    True _X_   False __

2. Theories of biological aging now provide us with adequate knowledge to begin experiments to reverse the aging process.

    True __   False _X_

3. Because of changes in the gastrointestinal system with aging, older people should eat two large meals daily instead of several smaller meals.

    True __   False _X_

4. Wound healing takes place more slowly in older people.

    True _X_   False __

5. Osteoporosis is a normal change in the musculoskeletal system with aging.

    True __   False _X_

6. Normal aging is accompanied by a slight increase in systolic blood pressure.

    True _X_   False __

7. Changes in the kidneys with aging indicate a need to increase the dosage of medications that are metabolized by the kidneys.

    True __   False _X_

8. Changes in the size and function of the liver with aging result in greater sensitivity to medications that are metabolized by the liver.

    True _X_   False __

9. Older people should reduce their intake of caffeine and alcohol because these substances inhibit the production of ADH.

    True _X_   False __

10. Neuronal loss with aging is the primary reason for older people's forgetfulness.

   True__   False X

11. Generally, older adults report that they sleep longer and deeper than when they were younger.

   True__   False X

12. Changes in circadian rhythms with aging appear to be associated with changes in core body temperatures.

   True X   False__

CHAPTER 6: SENSORY CHANGES AND THEIR SOCIAL CONSEQUENCES

Key Terms

Intraindividual changes

Interindividual differences

Sensation

Perception

Sensory threshold

Sensory discrimination

Refraction

Peripheral vision

Central vision

Glaucoma

Cataracts

Macular degeneration

Dark adaptation

Presbycusis

Tinnitus

Direct scaling techniques

Taste intensity

Olfactory acuity

Somesthetic sensitivity

Pain perception

Kinesthetic sensitivity

Environmental adaptation

Topics for Discussion

1. Provide three examples of normal, age-related changes in visual functioning and three examples of pathological aging. To what extent can environmental interventions aid the older person undergoing these changes?

2. There are numerous structural changes in the eye and the ear with aging that may influence older people's visual and auditory functioning. Describe these structural changes, and explain to what extent these changes versus changes in central processes may affect visual and auditory functioning.

3. To what extent does hearing loss affect personality in old age, as opposed to a co-existing change occurring in both areas?

4. Describe some communication techniques and environmental interventions that may be used by professionals working with older people who have hearing and vision impairments.

5. There is some debate about the role of structural changes versus social behavior in older people's complaints about their taste and olfactory acuity. Present evidence for each set of factors regarding their impact on older people's enjoyment of food and fragrances.

6. Discuss the importance of using more refined measurement techniques to assess age-related changes in taste and olfaction.

7.	To what extent are complaints of pain an indication of changes in tactile sensitivity vs. personality and social expectations among older persons?

8.	Discuss the impact of multiple sensory impairments occurring simultaneously on the need to modify an older person's physical environment.

Multiple Choice

1. Older people often have more problems seeing under low lighting conditions. This is most likely due to:

    a.   a reduction in the maximum opening of the pupil
    b.   a slower shift from rods to cones
    c.   a reduced supply of oxygen to the retina
    d.   none of the above
  X e.   all of the above

2. A common cause of vision loss among older persons that <u>can</u> be surgically corrected is:

  X a.   cataracts
    b.   senile macular degeneration
    c.   diabetic retinopathy
    d.   glaucoma

3. Collagen tissue changes the composition and elasticity of the lens with aging. This results in problems with:

    a.   visual acuity
    b.   peripheral vision
  X c.   accommodation
    d.   depth perception

4. Glaucoma results in increased problems with _____, whereas macular degeneration impairs _____.

  X a.   peripheral vision/central vision
    b.   central vision/peripheral vision
    c.   accommodation/acuity
    d.   color perception/discrimination

5. The best strategy for an older person who is experiencing age-related problems with vision is to:

    a.   see a psychiatrist
    b.   stop participating in activities outside the house
  X c.   modify the home environment to make it congruent with changing needs
    d.   turn to friends and relatives who can take over some responsibilities at home

6. With aging, there is increased difficulty in distinguishing between:

X   a. blue and green
      b. green and orange
      c. red and yellow
      d. red and orange

7. The structural change with aging that is most associated with hearing loss takes place in:

      a. the pinna
X   b. the cochlea
      c. the stapes
      d. the middle ear

8. Age-related hearing loss results in problems with all of the following functions except:

      a. hearing high frequency sounds
      b. distinguishing among sibilants
X   c. hearing low frequency sounds
      d. distinguishing background noises from relevant information

9. A major reason why many older people avoid using hearing aids is:

X   a. they raise the volume of background noises
      b. they make it difficult to hear oneself talk
      c. they are a problem to keep clean
      d. they are unattractive

10. Recent research on taste threshold sensitivity and aging has revealed that:

      a. taste thresholds in all four taste qualities increase with age
      b. taste thresholds in all four taste qualities decline with age
X   c. threshold loss does not occur in all taste qualities
      d. threshold loss is less of a problem for elderly than loss of taste intensity

11. Olfactory sensitivity in aging:

      a. deteriorates significantly
      b. shows greater decline than taste acuity
X   c. is retained among people with good olfactory sensitivity in their youth
      d. declines because of a significant reduction in the number of olfactory receptors

12. Increased complaints of pain among older people are:

X   a. often a sign of depression
      b. due to a lower threshold for pain with aging
      c. due to a higher threshold for pain with aging
      d. a normal concomitant of aging

13. All of the following factors may make it more difficult for an older person to drive a car except:

      a. arthritis
      b. decreased peripheral vision
      c. slower reaction time
X   d. inability to make decisions

14. An older person who is experiencing gradual declines in vision, hearing, taste and olfactory acuity simultaneously should do the following:

      a. seek medical intervention to solve the problem
      b. stop driving
X   c. substitute new activities that maintain P-E congruence
      d. move into a retirement home where others can cook and do household tasks

15. When conversing with an older adult with hearing loss, which of the following communication techniques is not likely to be helpful?

      a. using clear distinct articulation
X   b. speaking in a loud, high pitched voice
      c. sitting on the side of the person so you may talk into their good ear
      d. using short sentences

16. The kinesthetic system appears to change with aging, such that older people:

      a. become confused with visual cues
X   b. need more visual and surface cues
      c. prefer walking faster
      d. have difficulty with their tactile sensitivity

17. An older person who is experiencing problems with depth perception could improve their home environment by:

X   a. using color contrast where different levels meet
         b. using bright patterns on carpets throughout the house
         c. avoiding dark colors
         d. putting signs at the top of every stairway

18. An older person who complains that food does not taste as good as it did:

         a. is probably responding to the effects of medication
         b. should be told that this is an unavoidable part of aging
         c. should be encouraged to add more salt to food
X   d. should be encouraged to use herbs and spices liberally

True or False

1. Sensation is the process of receiving and processing information that has been received through the sense organs.

   True__   False _X_

2. The minimum intensity needed to discriminate between stimuli is greater than the intensity needed to recognize a stimulus.

   True _X_   False__

3. Increased consumption of carrots in old age can improve night vision.

   True__   False _X_

4. Arcus senilis can lead to blindness if not treated immediately.

   True__   False _X_

5. The best replacement lens for an older person who has had a cataract is a contact lens.

   True__   False _X_

6. Increased problems with glare are generally attributable to uneven hardening of the lens.

   True _X_   False__

7. Glaucoma is both more prevalent and more difficult to treat in African Americans.

   True _X_   False__

8. Tinnitus is a common condition among older people that can result in permanent deafness.

   True__   False _X_

9. When speaking to an older person with some hearing loss, it is useful to speak very slowly and exaggerate every syllable.

   True__   False _X_

10. Some psychiatric disorders have been found to result from severe hearing loss in older people.

   True___   False _X_

11. Contrary to earlier studies of taste and aging, recent researchers have found little evidence of taste bud loss with aging.

   True _X_   False___

12. Recent studies of taste acuity among older people have shown only minimal changes in taste thresholds for most of the primary tastes.

   True _X_   False___

13. The kinesthetic system is one of the few sensory functions that remain intact with aging.

   True___   False _X_

14. Researchers have found that increased pain thresholds with age are often attributable to psychological concerns.

   True _X_   False___

CHAPTER 7: HEALTH, CHRONIC DISEASES, AND USE OF HEALTH SERVICES

Key Terms

Osteoporosis
Activities of daily living
Disability
Quality of life
Chronic diseases
Acute diseases
Heart disease
  Arteriosclerosis
  Atherosclerosis
  Infarct
  Myocardial infarction
  Congestive heart failure
  Hypertension
  Hypotension
Stroke(Cerebrovascular accident)
Arthritis
  Rheumatoid arthritis
evaluations
  Osteoarthritis
  Contractures

Emphysema
Diabetes mellitus
Cystitis
Incontinence
  Stress
  Chronic functional
Diverticulitis
Hiatus hernia
Edentulism
AIDS
Accidents
Models of health behavior
  Behavioral model
  Health belief model
Congruence model
  Health promotion
  Subjective vs. objective health

Risk factors

Topics for Discussion

1. What are some of the implications of current research findings for the relationship between particular risk factors and illness?

2. If you were developing a health promotion program to encourage older people to visit physicians for preventive purposes, what model of health behavior would you utilize? Briefly describe the major components of your health promotion program.

3. Discuss how socio-cultural factors (demographics, cultural values) influence:

    a. evaluations of health
    b. health status
    c. health behavior
    d. utilization of health care services

4. If you were developing a health promotion program for individuals over age 75, what would be the major components of your program?

Multiple Choice

1. Compared to people aged 65 to 74, those 85 and older are almost ____ times more likely to need assistance in their activities of daily living.

    a. 2
X   b. 4
    c. 8
    d. 10

2. Most older people perceive their own health as ____ the health of their peers.
X   a. better than
    b. about the same
    c. worse than
    d. much worse than

3. Self-evaluations of health are most influenced by:

X   a. limitations in ADLs and number of meds used
    b. number of chronic illnesses and meds
    c. living at home vs. in a nursing home
    d. none of the above
    e. all of the above

4. Which of the following statements is true?

    a. The incidence of acute and chronic disease increases with age.
X   b. The incidence of acute diseases decreases with age.
    c. Men have more chronic conditions than women.
    d. Biological factors play almost no role in gender differences related to health.
    e. none of the above

5. The most common chronic condition among persons age 65 and over is:

    a. arteriosclerosis
    b. hypertension
    c. hearing impairments
X   d. arthritis

6. Which of the following is <u>not</u> true of chronic health conditions?

      a. Most older people have at least one.
X   b. They are short-term.
      c. The cause is usually unknown.
      d. Cures are currently not available.

7. Chronic illnesses are more prevalent and more disabling among:

      a. whites compared to nonwhites
      b. elders in cities compared to rural areas
      c. older people of higher socioeconomic status
X   d. women

8. Older African Americans have a disproportionately high incidence of:

      a. arteriosclerosis
X   b. hypertension
      c. cerebrovascular disease
      d. osteoporosis

9. The major cause of death among people age 65 and older is:

X   a. heart disease
      b. cancer
      c. stroke
      d. accidents and suicide

10. The major risk factor for cardiovascular disease is:

      a. hypotension
X   b. hypertension
      c. atherosclerosis
      d. diabetes

11. Osteoporosis is a major risk factor for:

      a. significant weight loss in older people
      b. problems with bladder control
X   c. hip fractures
      d. strokes

12. Osteoporosis occurs among:

    a. women only
    b. people over age 80 only
    c. men only
X   d. mostly women after the menopause

13. Currently the recommended methods of preventing osteoporosis include all <u>except</u>:

X   a. hormone replacement therapy after age 65
    b. hormone replacement therapy begun during menopause
    c. synthetic salmon calcitonin
    d. increased calcium intake ($\geq$ 1200mg) after age 40

14. Older people with incontinence:

    a. cannot be treated
X   b. should be examined for reversible causes
    c. can generally be treated with medications only
    d. consume more fluids

15. The primary cause of AIDS in people over age 70 today is:

X   a. blood transfusions
    b. homosexual contact
    c. heterosexual contact
    d. still unknown

16. Compared to young adults, older persons:

    a. are less likely to be victims of pedestrian accidents
    b. are less likely to die from injuries sustained in an accident
X   c. have more auto accidents per mile driven
    d. have more accidents due to drunken driving

17. Older people use dental services:

    a. as frequently as do younger age groups
X   b. much less frequently than any other age group
    c. mostly for preventive care
    d. frequently because they are covered by Medicare

18. National surveys of physician use in the United States reveal that people over age 65 are _____ more likely to visit a physician within one year than people in younger age groups:

   a. twice
   b. three times
X c. slightly
   d. significantly

19. All of the following are reasons why older people do not seek medical care for chronic conditions <u>except</u>:

X a. older people's lower likelihood of experiencing such illnesses
   b. physicians' attitudes about diseases of aging
   c. older people's attitudes about diseases of aging
   d. older people's concern about the costs of diagnostic tests and medical care

20. A model of health behavior that emphasizes the importance of modifying the health delivery system to encourage people to seek care is:

   a. the behavioral model
   b. the health belief model
X c. the congruence model
   d. the health promotion model

21. A model of health behavior that considers the effects of predisposing, enabling, and need variables is:

   a. the health belief model
X b. the behavioral model
   c. the congruence model
   d. none of the above

22. Risk factors for falls include all of the following except:

   a. inactivity
   b. visual impairments
   c. meds that can cause postural hypotension
X d. overexertion

23. All of the following are limitations of health promotion programs with the elderly except:

   a. most health promotion efforts have been short-term demonstration projects
   b. most health promotion programs have focused on the well population
   c. funding for continuing such programs is limited
X d. most health promotion programs encourage older people to seek more medical services than they would otherwise

True or False

1. Older people are likely to spend more days of restricted activity due to acute conditions than middle-aged people because they experience more incidents of acute disease.

   True _____   False _X_

2. Activities of daily living is a diagnostic category for types of diseases that have a high incidence among the elderly.

   True _____   False _X_

3. A factor that appears to be significantly related to life satisfaction is perceptions of one's health.

   True _X_   False _____

4. Significant increases in blood pressure are a universal corollary of aging.

   True _____   False _X_

5. Cerebrovascular accident (CVA) refers to a type of heart attack.

   True _____   False _X_

6. The most important treatment for arthritis is to limit any physical activity.

   True _____   False _X_

7. The symptoms of diabetes are difficult to detect in older people.

   True _X_   False _____

8. The most common form of diabetes in older people is one that develops late and can be managed without medication.

   True _X_   False _____

9. Stress incontinence is best treated with medications.

   True _____   False _X_

10. Constipation is a normal part of the aging process.

   True _____   False __X__

11. Older people may be more vulnerable to AIDS then younger persons because the immune system deteriorates with aging.

   True __X__   False _____

12. Because older people are aware of their risk of contracting AIDS, they are more likely to use condoms than younger adults.

   True _____   False __X__

13. There is little that we can do in our personal health practices to alter our active life expectancy.

   True _____   False __X__

14. Health promotion programs should attempt to improve the general environment as well as individual health practices.

   True __X__   False _____

15. Health promotion is not viable with frail older persons.

   True _____   False __X__

16. Older people who are injured in auto accidents have a greater risk of hospitalization and death than young persons.

   True __X__   False _____

CHAPTER 8: COGNITIVE CHANGES WITH AGING

Key Terms

General factor theory
Structure of intelligence
Intelligence quotient (IQ)
Fluid intelligence
Crystallized intelligence
Wechsler Adult Intelligence Scale (WAIS)
Classic Aging Pattern
Primary mental abilities
Terminal drop hypothesis
Selective attrition
Errors of omission
Errors of commission

Learning
Memory
Sensory memory
  Iconic memory
  Echoic memory
Primary memory
Secondary memory
Spatial memory
Information processing model
Mnemonics
Method of loci
Creativity
Divergent thinking

Topics for Discussion

1. Discuss examples of changes in crystallized and fluid intelligence with aging. In what ways could methodological problems result in exaggerating declines in these two types of intelligence?

2. Discuss the advantages and disadvantages of longitudinal research designs to study intelligence in old age.

3. To what extent do changes in sensory processes and physiological functioning affect older people's memory at the stages of sensory, primary and secondary memory?

4. In what ways can the learning environment be enhanced to improve learning ability and retention of newly acquired information in the older learner? What factors can disrupt older people's acquisition of new information?

5. Studies of learning among younger people have found an inverse U-function between anxiety and performance, such that a moderate level of anxiety is associated with optimal learning. To what extent does this model apply to older learners?

6. In what ways have older persons been found to compensate for declines in information processing and perceptual-motor speed?

Multiple Choice

1. All of the following represent dimensions in Guilford's model of intellect except:

    a. operations
    b. content
X   c. performance
    d. products

2. Two models of intelligence that include a general intelligence factor are those proposed by:

    a. Guilford and Spearman
    b. Cattell and Guilford
    c. Cattell and Thurstone & Thurstone
X   d. Spearman and Thurstone & Thurstone

3. The component of intelligence that consists of skills acquired through a lifetime of experiences and education is known as:

    a. fluid intelligence
X   b. crystallized intelligence
    c. primary mental abilities
    d. omnibus intelligence

4. The classic aging pattern is the term used to describe:

    a. decline on all subtests of the WAIS after age 50
    b. decline on verbal scales of the WAIS after age 60
X   c. decline on performance scales of the WAIS after age 65
    d. improvement on the WAIS between 55 and 75, with a significant drop after 75

5. Selective attrition from longitudinal studies of intellectual functioning often results in the inaccurate conclusion that:

X   a. intellectual functioning remains stable or improves over time.
    b. intellectual functioning declines significantly over time.
    c. older people who volunteer for studies of intelligence are the least healthy.
    d. older people who survive in these studies are slower than others.

6. A major longitudinal study of intelligence in older persons that has resulted in the development of sequential research designs is the:

    a. New York State Study of Twins
    b. Iowa State Study
X   c. Seattle Longitudinal Study
    d. Duke Longitudinal Studies

7. Adult intelligence appears to be influenced by:

    a. education
    b. health
    c. initial level of intelligence
X   d. all of the above
    e. none of the above

8. Performance on tests of intelligence by older persons with hypertension, compared to those with normal blood pressure, is:

X   a. worse
    b. better
    c. about the same
    d. has not been tested

9. The decline in intelligence test scores just before death is known as:

    a. selective attrition
    b. psychomotor slowing
X   c. terminal drop
    d. retrieval abilities

10. The process of encoding new information into one's memory is known as:

X   a. learning
    b. intelligence
    c. iconic memory
    d. sensory memory

11. New information first enters a temporary storage for 1/10 second or less. This is known as:
    a. primary memory
    b. spatial memory
    c. iconic memory
X   d. sensory memory

12.   Studies of primary memory in older people have found:

      a. they can recall less than 4 pieces of information
X   b. they can recall 7 ± 2 pieces of information
      c. significantly poorer recall than among younger persons
      d. much better short-term recall than long-term recall

13.   Older adults do better on tests:

      a. when given an opportunity to guess
      b. under timed learning situations
X   c. under self-paced conditions
      d. when the stakes are high

14.   All of the following conditions help older learners except:

X   a. a verbal challenge that the test reveals their intelligence
      b. a supportive test condition
      c. positive feedback
      d. conducting the learning tests under real world conditions

15.   Age related deficiencies have been found in tests of_____, but not in tests of
      _____.

      a. recognition/recall
X   b. recall/recognition
      c. primary memory/secondary memory
      d. distant events/recent events

16.   Studies of typing skill in typists ranging from age 19 to 72 have revealed all the
      following changes with age except that older typists:

      a. have slower reaction time than young typists
      b. can complete the task in the same time as young typists
X   c. cannot compensate for slower perceptual-motor speed
      d. make more efficient moves on the task

17. Associating new information with an image has been found to be useful for older people as a:

     a. method of finding their way around a new place
     b. method of enhancing creativity
     c. way of remembering where they have placed their belongings
X   d. method of visualizing newly learned words or concepts

18. Studies of wisdom and creativity with aging:

     a. reveal increased abilities in these areas as the person ages
     b. reveal declining abilities in these areas as the person ages
X   c. are currently not widely available
     d. have generally used tests of convergent thinking

True or False

1. It is generally agreed by researchers that most types of intelligence decline after age 60.

   True _____   False _X_

2. Studies of health status and performance on tests of intelligence reveal greater decline among those with high blood pressure.

   True _X_   False _____

3. Researchers have found inconsistent results regarding the ability to use abstract thought processes in old age.

   True _X_   False _____

4. Declines in the ability to perform some intelligence tests by the elderly have been found to be due primarily to slower reaction time with age.

   True _____   False _X_

5. The Seattle Longitudinal Study has demostrated that, by age 80, there is a significant decline for most people in all five primary mental abilities.

   True _____   False _X_

6. Older subjects make more errors of omission than errors of commission in tests of paired associates.

   True _X_   False _____

7. Long-term memory appears to deteriorate with aging because of information overload.

   True _____   False _X_

8. Older persons perform better than younger subjects when given the chance to give creative responses under conditions of uncertainty and high risk.

   True _____   False _X_

9. Older subjects perform much worse than younger persons on tests of free recall.

   True _X_   False _____

10. Age differences in spatial memory persist, even with multiple visual cues.

    True _____   False _X_

11. Researchers who have measured creative output by artists at different ages have found that output declines linearly after age 60.

    True _____   False _X_

12. Older people are more likely than younger persons to have achieved wisdom because of their greater opportunities to integrate life experiences.

    True _X_   False _____

CHAPTER 9: PERSONALITY AND SOCIAL ADAPTATION IN OLD AGE

Key Terms

Nature vs. nurture
Stages of development
Epigenetic principle
Archetypes
Subjective well-being
Active mastery
Passive mastery
Kansas City studies
Individuation
Stress
Coping
Ego defense mechanisms
Adaptation
Role gains and losses

Personality types
   Integrated
   Armored-defensive
   Passive-dependent
   Disorganized (unintegrated)
Successful aging
Dialectical models
Life structure
Moral development
Self-concept
Self-esteem
Life-review
Life events
   On-time vs off-time events
   Cognitive appraisal
   Life change units

Topics for Discussion

1. Discuss the contributions of the Kansas City Studies of Aging to our understanding of personality in old age and to research methods in social gerontology.

2. Dialectical models of personality are consistent with the person-environment perspective used throughout this book. Describe how Levinson's and Riegel's theories apply this dynamic approach to personality development in old age.

3. Self-concept is generally established early in life, but is modified through social roles and life experiences. Discuss some experiences of the later years that may affect an older person's self-concept and that may negatively influence their self-esteem.

4. Cognitive appraisal has been suggested as a modifier of the perceived stressfulness of a life event. Other researchers have noted that life events are stressful by their very nature. Provide arguments supporting and opposing each position.

5. Discuss the advantages and disadvantages of using a standard life events rating scale developed with younger persons in research with older persons.

6. Describe the major differences between ego defense mechanisms and coping styles. Which types of defense mechanisms and coping styles would one expect to be utilized by older people?

7. Discuss the qualities that result in "successful aging." How can health promotion help older people achieve a successful old age?

Multiple Choice

1. Among the following factors, our personalities are influenced most by:

   X   a.   the social environment
         b.   gender
         c.   the weather
         d.   expectations about rewards and punishment

2. The final crisis faced by the individual in Erik Erikson's theory of personality is known as:

         a.   ego identity vs. role diffusion
   X   b.   ego integrity vs. despair
         c.   intimacy vs. isolation
         d.   generativity vs. stagnation

3. A major difference between Freud and personality theorists who focus on adult development is that Freud:

         a.   emphasized development throughout the life cycle
         b.   discouraged the view that development proceeds through specific stages
         c.   focused on psychosocial development
   X   d.   suggests that personality is developed by adolescence

4. A theory of personality that emphasizes the importance of inner exploration in the later years has been advanced by:

         a.   Erik Erikson
         b.   Daniel Levinson
         c.   David Gutmann
   X   d.   Carl Jung

5. There is decreased sex role stereotyping with aging, according to:

         a.   Gutmann
         b.   Jung
         c.   Neugarten
   X   d.   All of the above
         e.   None of the above

6. The Kansas City studies have revealed that aging is associated with:

      a. increased extroversion
X   b. greater differentiation
      c. greater risk-taking
      d. an increase in conservative beliefs

7. High life satisfaction has been found among older people who may be described as:

X   a. the integrated type
      b. using magical mastery styles
      c. the unintegrated type
      d. the constricted elderly

8. Which of the following theories or models of personality development does not take a dialectical approach?

X   a. Jung's
      b. Erikson's
      c. Levinson's
      d. Riegel's

9. Kohlberg's theory suggests that the sixth stage of moral development will be achieved:

      a. by most people in their 20's
      b. by most older people
X   c. by relatively few people
      d. through religious involvement

10. Which of the following theories of personality development is not associated with chronological age?

X   a. Kohlberg's
      b. Erikson's
      c. Levinson's
      d. Neugarten's

11. Older people whose self-concept is closely associated with the roles they held when younger:

      a. generally adjust more readily to aging
X   b. usually have more difficulty adapting to aging
      c. cope well with off-time events
      d. have higher self-esteem than other older people

12. Comparisons in life change units assigned by younger and older people reveal:

      a.   considerable similarity in absolute scores
      b.   similarity in the events rated as positive stressors
X   c.   similarity in the relative stress of many items
      d.   higher scores assigned by people who have experienced the event

13. Compared to younger persons who have not experienced a particular life event, older people:

      a.   assign a higher life change unit to the event
X   b.   assign it a lower life change unit
      c.   report that it was not stressful
      d.   report using 1-2 coping responses to it.

14. All of the following may determine older people's reaction to a life event except:

      a.   their cognitive appraisal of the situation
      b.   the availability of a strong social network
X   c.   chronological age
      d.   locus of control

15. Adults are more likely than children to use the defense mechanism of:

      a.   denial
      b.   projection
      c.   emotional expression
X   d.   sublimation

16. Many studies have found that coping responses among older people tend to be:

      a.   more passive and ineffective than among the young
X   b.   variable according to the situation
      c.   more constricted than among the young
      d.   determined by their physical health

17. Older people who age successfully have been found to have all the following characteristics except:

X   a.   high on financial independence
      b.   independence in ADL's
      c.   high on tests of mental status
      d.   healthy lifestyles

18. Successful aging implies that the older person:

    a. has survived to old age
    b. has achieved ego integrity
X   c. has adapted well to many different events
    d. uses health services more than average

True or False

1. Most people experience maladaptive personality shifts as they age.

    True _____   False _X_

2. The Kansas City studies found that people become more alike as they age.

    True _____   False _X_

3. Socialization into old age is easy for most people because of the widespread availability of successful role models.

    True _____   False _X_

4. Cognitive appraisal of a life event aids us in determining its relative stressfulness.
    True _X_   False _____

5. Both men and women move toward greater femininity as they age.

    True _____   False _X_

6. Differences in readjustment scores assigned to the same life event by people who have and have not experienced the event suggest that the anticipation of many events may be more stressful than their actual occurrence.

    True _X_   False _____

7. There is considerable research evidence that most normative events, such as the death of one's spouse in old age, result in less stress than non-normative events.

    True _____   False _X_

8. Older people are even more likely than the young to use mature coping styles in a given situation.

    True _X_   False _____

9. Defense mechanisms and coping strategies may both be defined as unconscious means of adapting to stressful situations.

    True _____   False _X_

10. Levinson's "life structures" are analogous to Erikson's stages of ego development.

    True _____   False _X_

11. Kohlberg's model of human development does not postulate stages that occur chronologically, nor that a smooth progression through stages necessarily occurs.

    True _X_   False _____

12. Major longitudinal studies of successful aging have generally found that even this group of older people have multiple chronic diseases.

    True _____   False _X_

13. "Robust elders" in the MacArthur and Manitoba studies were more likely to report themselves in good health, despite having multiple health problems.

    True _____   False _X_

14. Adaptation to old age is easier for those with good coping skills.

    True _X_   False _____

CHAPTER 10: LOVE, INTIMACY, AND SEXUALITY IN OLD AGE

Key Terms

Sexuality
Estrogen
Progesterone
Menopause
  Premenopause
  Postmenopause
  Climacteric
  Hot flashes
  Hormone replacement therapy
Male climacteric

Testosterone
Impotence
Gay and lesbian partners
Performance anxiety
Widower's syndrome
Widow's syndrome

Topics for Discussion

1. What are the prevalent attitudes and beliefs about sex and love in old age? Discuss how these are reflected in our society and what consequences they have for older adults.

2. What are the major factors that affect sexual activity in older adults?

3. Discuss the primary physiological changes that are experienced by men and women and the implications for sexual response, performance and pleasure.

4. How can professionals assist older men and women to adapt to age-related changes that will enhance their experiences with intimacy and their sexual functioning and enjoyment?

5. In what ways do nursing homes deny the sexual needs of residents? What can nursing home staff do to respect the sexual needs of older residents?

6. What are particular issues that older gay men and lesbians face in our society? If you were a health care professional, how would you try to address these issues in working with older homosexual couples?

Multiple Choice

1. The early research on sexuality of older adults was limited in all of the following ways <u>except</u> for:

      a.   an emphasis on frequency of sexual intercourse
      b.   the nonrepresentative nature of samples
      c.   comparisons of younger and older cohorts
X   d.   longitudinal research designs

2. The climacteric is:

      a.   a medicine for treating sexual dysfunction
X   b.   a decline in sexual hormone levels resulting in a loss or reduction of reproductive ability.
      c.   a hormone
      d.   a stage of sexual functioning

3. In old age, sexual feelings:

      a.   continue only if they are acted upon
X   b.   can be expressed in ways other than genital contact
      c.   are inappropriate
      d.   normally fade away

4. Which of the following physiological conditions are related to the decrease in estrogen in menopausal and postmenopausal women:

      a.   hot flashes
      b.   genital atrophy
      c.   urinary tract changes
      d.   bone changes
X   e.   all of the above

5. A danger of hormone replacement therapy for some older women is:

      a.   diminished sexual response
      b.   a higher risk of heart disease
      c.   more painful intercourse
X   d.   increased risk of uterine cancer

6. A recent positive change in the treatment of menopause is:

       a.   use of prescription drugs
X   b.   the increased use of nonmedical approaches and social support
       c.   use of estrogen
       d.   none of the above
       e.   all of the above

7. Which of the following is true?

       a.   Older males enjoy sex more than older females.
X   b.   The male climacteric comes later and progresses at a slower rate than the female climacteric.
       c.   Women's capacity for orgasm is severely impaired after the age of 65.
       d.   none of the above

8. Which of the following is true about older lesbians?

       a.   They are less fearful of changes in appearance than heterosexual women.
       b.   Most remain sexually active as they age.
       c.   They usually report a positive self-image.
X   d.   all of the above
       e.   none of the above

9. Which of the following is <u>not</u> true about older gay men?

       a.   They are more concerned about their physical appearance than are lesbian women.
       b.   They generally maintain positive feelings about their looks.
X   c.   Most are lonely and depressed.
       d.   all of the above

10. Which of the following conditions are common causes of impotence in older males?

       a.   prolonged alcoholism
       b.   diabetes
       c.   arthritis
X   d.   a and b
       e.   a and c

11. Aging alters men's sexual functioning by:

      a.   making them impotent
      b.   creating a loss of interest in sexual activity
      c.   reducing the time between orgasm and subsequent erection
X   d.   increasing the time between orgasm and subsequent erection

12. Which of the following is true?

      a.   Little sexual pleasure is possible for males with irreversible impotence.
X   b.   A major barrier for older women to be sexually active is lack of a partner.
      c.   Tranquilizers heighten sexual performance.
      d.   Older men ejaculate more quickly.

13. In instances where an older person conveys concern about his/her sexuality to a health care provider, which of the following is not an appropriate professional response?

      a.   Determine whether drugs are affecting sexual performance
X   b.   Tell the older person that he/she should no longer worry about sexual responsiveness
      c.   Screen for any disease-related causes of changes in sexual responsiveness
      d.   all of the above
      e.   none of the above

14. Which of the following statements about sexual activity in late adulthood is true?

      a.   The major barrier for men is lack of a partner.
      b.   There are physiological limits to how long women can be sexually active.
X   c.   The most important factor in maintaining sexuality is consistent sexual activity throughout middle and late adulthood.
      d.   all of the above
      e.   none of the above

15. Widower's syndrome is a condition that may occur in older males who:

X   a.   have refrained from sexual activity for an extended period of time following their wife's death
      b.   have intense and frequent sexual activity following their wife's death
      c.   are terrified of their wife's death
      d.   none of the above

16. Sexual expression can assume more significance in old age if:

      a.   nursing homes provide privacy
      b.   doctors avoid prescribing drugs that interfere with sexuality
      c.   younger people do not ridicule older people's sexual feelings
X   d.   all of the above

17. Sexuality refers to:

      a.   an energy force expressed in every aspect of being
      b.   a person's speech, movement, vitality and ability to enjoy life
      c.   the expression of feelings and self in an intimate way
X   d.   all of the above

18. When visiting an older person in a nursing home, the most important type of sensory stimulation that a visitor might provide is:

      a.   wearing bright colored clothing
X   b.   touching the older person (such as backrubs, holding hands)
      c.   feeding the older person
      d.   wearing cologne

True or False

1. Sexuality often continues to be an important part of relationships in late adulthood.

    True __X__   False _____

2. Most older individuals do not engage in sexual intercourse.

    True _____   False _X_

3. Reanalysis of the 1954 Duke Longitudinal Study data found older women to be more interested in sex than older men.

    True __X__   False _____

4. Over 50% of married persons age 60 and older report having sex about four times a month.

    True __X__   False _____

5. Physiological, age-related changes can affect the nature of the sexual response.

    True __X__   False _____

6. In women, menopause is considered to have occurred when two consecutive months have passed without a menstrual period.

    True _____   False _X_

7. The majority of older women experience only mild menopausal symptoms.

    True __X__   False _____

8. Only a very small percentage of women experience hot flashes during menopause.
    True _____   False _X_

9. The majority of older women experience and enjoy orgasms.

    True __X__   False _____

10. Prostate surgery inevitably results in irreversible impotence.

    True _____   False _X_

11. Impotence, the most common sexual disorder among older men, is always caused by physiological factors.

   True _____   False _X_

12. For the current cohort of older people, most sexual activity occurs within the context of the marital relationship.

   True _X_   False _____

13. Frail nursing home residents have little need for sexual intimacy.

   True _____   False _X_

14. Sex therapy with older adults should emphasize ways to maintain genital intercourse.

   True _____   False _X_

15. During late adulthood, sex and love are more important than at any other time of life.

   True _____   False _X_

CHAPTER 11: MENTAL DISORDERS AND THE USE OF MENTAL HEALTH SERVICES

Key Terms

Late life psychopathology
Depression
  Major depression
  Secondary (reactive)
  Unipolar/bipolar
  Masked
  Pseudo-dementia
Electroconvulsive therapy (ECT)
Dementia
  Reversible
  Irreversible
  Alzheimer's disease
  Multi-infarct dementia

Nerve growth factor
Amyloid
Apolipoprotein (apo-E)
Global deterioration scale
Schizophrenia
Paraphrenia
Paranoia
Life review
Group therapy
Reality orientation
Remotivation therapy
Caregiver stress
Chronically mentally ill

Topics for Discussion

1. Prevalence rates vary widely for major psychiatric disorders among the elderly, especially among ethnic minority elderly. Describe some reasons why it is difficult to obtain accurate figures for these conditions in the older population.

2. In what ways, if any, is depression manifested in older people? What types of depression are most common in this group? Which therapeutic interventions appear to be most successful in treating these forms of late life depression?

3. Discuss some of the new developments in research on dementia, especially the research on causes of Alzheimer's disease. What, if any, implications do these studies have for diagnosing and treating AD patients?

4. Discuss the range of therapeutic interventions that could be beneficial to Alzheimer's patients and to their family members.

5. Describe why alcoholism is often more difficult to detect in older people, and why therapeutic interventions are critical for older alcoholics.

6. Develop a mental health service delivery system that would best fit the needs of older people and that would be utilized by the majority of older people who need mental health services, including ethnic minority elderly.

Multiple Choice

1. The prevalence of psychiatric disorders among elderly in the community has been estimated to be:

      a.   50%
      b.   5%
X   c.   15 to 25%
      d.   20 to 80%

2. Which of the following statements regarding psychiatric disorders among ethnic minority elderly is true?

      a.   They are far less likely to experience psychiatric disorders than whites.
      b.   They use community mental health services more often than whites.
      c.   American Indians use psychiatric institutions more than whites.
X   d.   Prevalence data are not as widely available as for whites.

3. The most prevalent psychiatric disorder in old age is:

X   a.   depression
      b.   dementia
      c.   paranoia
      d.   schizophrenia

4. The most common form of depression in the later years is:

      a.   bipolar depression
X   b.   unipolar depression
      c.   grief reaction
      d.   reactive depression

5. DSM-III criteria for major depression in older people:

X   a.   are no different than for younger persons
      b.   include more vegetative symptoms
      c.   emphasize the greater likelihood of suicidal thoughts among depressed elderly
      d.   emphasize older people's greater likelihood of masking their depression

6. It is often difficult to diagnose depression in older people because:

    a. they show no symptoms
    b. they are more likely to complain of mood changes
X   c. they are more likely to have somatic and memory complaints
    d. they do not believe in the value of medical interventions for depression

7. The least effective therapy for older depressed persons is:

X   a. to do nothing
    b. antidepressant medications
    c. ECT
    d. psychotherapy

8. Suicide rates among different age and ethnic groups, and between men and women,:

    a. do not vary widely
    b. are highest in young males, lowest in white females
X   c. are highest among older white males, lowest in non-white females
    d. are highest among older Black males, lowest among white females

9. Older people are more likely than younger people to:

    a. discuss but never complete a suicide attempt
X   b. successfully carry out a suicide
    c. seek psychiatric help to prevent a suicide
    d. provide many cues about an impending suicide

10. Dementia in old age:

    a. is a natural accompaniment to the aging process
    b. generally is irreversible
X   c. should first be examined for reversible causes
    d. most often manifests itself as a personality disorder

11. The diagnosis of Alzheimer's disease:

    a. is straightforward because of distinctive symptoms
    b. can be made most accurately through psychological testing
    c. is different from any other form of dementia
X   d. is most accurate at autopsy

12. There is considerable research evidence currently to conclude that Alzheimer's disease is caused by:

      a.   a chromosomal defect
      b.   an accumulation of aluminum in the brain
      c.   a slow virus
X   d.   high levels of abnormal proteins in the brain

13. The region in the brain that appears to show the first signs of plaques and tangles is the _____; this is associated with early stage changes in _____ among Alzheimer's patients.

X   a.   hippocampus/learning and memory
      b.   locus ceruleus/anger
      c.   cerebral cortex/language
      d.   limbic system/movement

14. As the stress of caregiving has become increasingly recognized, which of the following has not emerged as a way to assist caregivers?

      a.   support groups
      b.   the ADRDA
X   c.   Medicare reimbursement for caregivers' psychotherapy
      d.   adult day care centers

15. Compared to younger persons, people over age 65:

      a.   are more likely to abuse drugs and alcohol
X   b.   are more likely to take prescription and over-the-counter drugs
      c.   are more likely to seek psychiatric help for alcoholism
      d.   are less likely to be affected by multiple medications

16. Long-term follow-ups of therapeutic interventions in nursing homes have found that the most effective intervention is:

      a.   reality orientation
      b.   remotivation therapy
      c.   cognitive behavioral strategies
      d.   none of the above because institutionalized elderly do not respond well
X   e.   none of the above has been followed for its long-term effects

17.   All of the following are barriers to older persons' seeking assistance for psychiatric symptoms <u>except</u>:

      a.   social stigmas about psychiatric disorders
X   b.   a preference for self-medication to treat the condition
      c.   mental health service providers' attitudes
      d.   attributions of the psychiatric symptoms to physical conditions

18.   The chronically mentally ill population:
X   a.   suffers from social disruption
      b.   includes very few elderly
      c.   consists of long-term drug addicts
      d.   gets regular psychotherapy

True or False

1. Depression in older people generally cannot be treated as well as depression in younger persons.

    True _____   False _X_

2. The prevalence rate for depression among older nursing home residents is much greater than among their counterparts still living in the community.

    True _X_   False _____

3. Recent statistics reveal a significant decline in suicide rates among older African American men.

    True _____   False _X_

4. There are more nonfatal suicides among older men than among the young.

    True _X_   False _____

5. Older people using multiple medications may, as a result, experience an irreversible dementia.

    True _____   False _X_

6. There is a significant difference between senile and presenile dementia in their symptoms and course.

    True _____   False _X_

7. It is as important to provide psychological support for families of dementia victims as for the patients themselves.

    True _X_   False _____

8. It is important to thoroughly screen patients with symptoms of dementia so that treatment for potential secondary causes may be undertaken.

    True _X_   False _____

9. Alcoholism is higher among older men than among middle-aged men.

    True _____   False _X_

10. Psychotherapy can be just as successful with older persons as it is with younger adults.

    True __X__   False _____

11. Older persons are far less likely to seek care in community mental health centers than in hospitals.

    True __X__   False _____

12. Older people are more likely to seek help for psychiatric conditions from a general physician than from mental health professionals.

    True __X__   False _____

13. Noncompliance with medication regimens is <u>not</u> a problem for older persons.

    True _____   False __X__

14. Chronically mentally ill older persons receive good medical care because local hospitals keep track of most of these people.

    True _____   False __X__

CHAPTER 12: THE IMPORTANCE OF SOCIAL SUPPORTS: FAMILY, FRIENDS, AND NEIGHBORS

Key Terms

Multigenerational family
Objective and subjective burden of caregiving
Intergenerational assistance
Blended or reconstituted families
Grandparents as caregivers
Gay and lesbian partners
"Intimacy at a distance"
"Women in the middle"
Older parents caring for children with chronic illness
Grandparents' rights

Family and Medicare Leave Act
Elder abuse
Social support interventions
Personal network building and natural helpers
Gate-keepers
Volunteer linking
Mutual help networks
Neighborhood and community development
Pets as emotional support

Topics for Discussion

1.   What do you think are some factors that explain the persistence of myths about the aging family in our culture?

2.   You have been asked to recommend policies and programs regarding family caregiving to your state legislature. Based upon the evidence regarding families' needs, what policy changes would you recommend? What would be the rationale for your recommendations?

3.   What are some steps that you could take now to ensure that you will have a strong informal support system in old age?

4.   What are some of the social and cultural factors that underlie why family caregivers of older adults (especially spouses) have tended to be ignored by practitioners and policy makers?

5.   Assume that you are the director of a retirement home where most residents are age 75 and over. What programs might you develop to foster intergenerational contacts?

6.   Assume that you are a counselor working with a four-generation family which is experiencing conflicts over caring for a great-grandparent. What would you do to encourage positive intergenerational exchanges? Specifically, what could be done to strengthen the grandchildren-grandparent interactions?

7. From the perspective of your discipline, describe an intervention(s) to strengthen an older person's social support system within a high rise apartment building for low-income elders.

8. What kinds of services and supports would you recommend for the growing numbers of grandparents who are assuming the primary care of grandchildren?

9. Discuss how ethnic minority status, socioeconomic class, gender and sexual orientation affect family roles and relationships for older people.

10. In what ways is the aging family of the future likely to be different from contemporary families?

11. If you were designing a training program on diversity for community home health care staff, what content would you include about families, including gay and lesbian partners?

Multiple Choice

1. Which of the following statements about the aging family is true?

   a. Most older persons live so geographically distant from their families that they do not regularly see any relatives.

   X   b. Family members provide the majority of in-home care to older relatives with functional disabilities.

   c. At the turn of the century, the majority of older people lived in multigenerational households.

   d. Most older people would prefer to live with their children and grandchildren.

2. In terms of living situation, most older adults live:

   a. in institutions

   b. alone

   X   c. with a spouse, children or other relatives

   d. with non-relatives

3. Studies of marital satisfaction across the lifespan show that marital satisfaction:

   a. decreases with length of time married

   b. decreases when children are being reared, and gets lower when children leave home

   X   c. is high among those recently married, lower during the childrearing period, and higher in later phases

   d. is high among those recently married and is lower when children leave home

4. Which of the following factors is least related to successful remarriages?

   X   a. partners being the same age

   b. partners having been friends prior to the remarriage

   c. approval of the marriage by family and friends

   d. adequate financial resources

5. Although research on older gay and lesbian partners is limited, we can conclude with reasonable certainty that:

   a. they are more satisfied in old age than their heterosexual peers.

   b. they are more concerned with physical appearance than their heterosexual peers.

   X   c. they face certain structural and legal barriers not encountered by their heterosexual peers.

   d. all of the above

6. Studies of older siblings indicate that:

    a. contacts among siblings are more frequent than among other relationships.
    b. few older persons have siblings alive.
    c. contact is greatest in middle age and then declines.
X   d. feelings of affection and closeness often increase with age.

7. There are many different myths about the aging family. Which of the following is not a myth?

    a. Most older adults have little contact with family members.
X   b. Most older people prefer not to live with their children, but instead like "intimacy at a distance."
    c. Older individuals usually become alienated from their children.
    d. Most families place their older relatives in nursing homes.

8. The primary source of emotional support for an older person generally is:

    a. neighbors
    b. clergy
X   c. family
    d. friends

9. Patterns of assistance among members of the multigenerational family are affected by:

    a. women's increased labor force participation
    b. geographic mobility of younger family members
    c. growing rates of divorce and remarriage
    d. the growth of frail older people
X   e. all of the above.

10. Studies of relationships between adult children and their older parents indicate:

X   a. most older parents see an adult child frequently
    b. most parents do not live geographically near to any of their children.
    c. most older parents are alienated from their children.
    d. most older parents rarely see their children.

11. Women compose nearly ____% of the family caregivers for older relatives with chronic illness

    a.   30
    b.   50
X   c.   80
    d.   none of the above

12. Older people who never married and are without children, and thus do not have adult children to care for them, are characterized as follows:

    a.   generally are more destitute than those with children
X   b.   usually develop other support systems and turn to others for help
    c.   are often much happier because adult children tend to let down their older parents
    d.   generally experience much worse health

13. The "sandwiched generation" is typically:

    a.   middle aged
    b.   responsible for providing care to at least two generations of dependents
    c.   juggling the roles of paid worker and caregiver to dependents
X   d.   all of the above
    e.   none of the above

14. The greatest burdens experienced by family caregivers to older persons are:

    a.   the costs of medical care
    b.   the physical demands of cooking and cleaning
X   c.   the emotional burdens of feeling alone and without time for oneself
    d.   the feeling that they are doing more than they should be

15. Middle-aged adult children are experiencing growing pressures to provide care to their older parents because:

    a.   the current cohort of older adults had fewer children than previous generations
    b.   the proportion of people age 85+ has grown more rapidly than any other age group
    c.   public funds for in-home care are limited
X   d.   all of the above
    e.   none of the above

16. The primary responsibility for meeting the needs of aging parents generally falls upon:

      a.   the oldest members of the family
      b.   the family member with the most money
X   c.   female members of the family
      d.   both sexes equally

17. Families' use of social and health services can be characterized as follows:

      a.   families turn readily to formal services
      b.   once services are available, families withdraw from providing care
X   c.   families use services selectively to supplement their own caregiving
      d.   none of the above.

18. Parents of adult children who are developmentally disabled or chronically mentally ill can be characterized as:

      a.   lacking adequate services
      b.   facing their own age-related changes
      c.   perpetual caregivers
X.   d.   all of the above
      e.   none of the above

19. Neglect or physical or psychological abuse of older family members is:

X   a.   most likely to be committed by a spouse who is the primary caregiver or by a son
      b.   probably over-reported
      c.   present in nearly all multigenerational families
      d.   all of the above

20. A major predictor of nursing home placement is:

      a.   the nature of the older person's illness
      b.   the older person's mental competence
      c.   the condition of the older person's home
X   d.   the family caregiver's physical and mental status and social supports

21. The primary factor that affects the frequency of visiting between grandparents and grandchildren is:

X   a.   geographic proximity
        b.   the gender of the grandparent and grandchild
        c.   whether or not parents and grandparents get along with one another
        d.   divorce

22. Friendship patterns in later life appear to be most strongly related to:

        a.   the type of assistance needed
        b.   similarity in terms of age and other characteristics
        c.   gender
        d.   length of neighborhood residence
X   e.   all of the above
        f.   none of the above

23. In their social relationships in later life, men tend to:

        a.   place more value on friendships than women do
        b.   be more aggressive about their friendships than women are
X   c.   depend on their wives for companionship
        d.   have a greater need for friends in later life than women do

24. Interventions with informal support systems aim to:

        a.   strengthen natural helping networks
        b.   enhance a group or community's problem-solving capacity
        c.   build upon natural helpers' interactions with older people
        d.   none of the above
X   e.   all of the above

True or False

1. Surveys have found that the most satisfied older persons are those who are married.
    True _X_   False _____

2. The largest category of single persons in the current cohort of older people is divorced persons.

    True _____   False _X_

3. Childless older adults with health problems tend to be more isolated than other older people are.

    True _X_   False _____

4. Divorce in later life is decreasing.

    True ___   False _X_

5. In terms of the proportion of older men and women who are married, there is a higher percentage of older married men than women.

    True _X_   False _____

6. Older men who are divorced have the least chance of remarriage.

    True _____   False _X_

7. The majority of older individuals live alone.

    True _____   False _X_

8. Having common interests and values is the most important factor in successful marriage in late adulthood.

    True _X_   False _____

9. Among siblings in old age, sisters are more likely to maintain family ties than are brothers.

    True _X_   False _____

10. Most studies indicate that the majority of adult children now reject the norm of filial responsibility (i.e., that adult children should help their parents).

    True _____   False _X_

11. Older parents typically receive help from their adult children but rarely are able to assist their children.

    True _____   False _X_

12. Multigenerational households tend to be more prevalent among ethnic minority families than in Caucasian families.

    True _X_   False _____

13. Formal institutions, such as day care centers and nursing homes, now provide more care than does the family.

    True _____   False _X_

14. Most families prefer nursing home placements over trying to maintain their older relatives at home.

    True _____   False _X_

15. The role of grandparent tends to be the most important one in an older person's life.

    True _____   False _X_

16. The majority of older people are grandparents and see a grandchild at least once a week.

    True _X_   False _____

17. Friends are often a more important source of support than family in old age because they are chosen.

    True _X_   False _____

18. Informal support systems have been found to be more important to older adults' well-being than formal support services.

    True _X_   False _____

CHAPTER 13: LIVING ARRANGEMENTS AND SOCIAL INTERACTIONS

Key Terms

Person-environment theories
   Personology
   Socioenvironmental theory
   Person-environment congruence
   Competence model
Age-homogeneity-heterogeneity
Fear-victimization paradox
Homesharing
Home equity conversion mortgages
Planned housing
Congregate housing
Multilevel facilities
Lifecare (lifelease) contracts

Environmental quality
   Privacy
   Accessibility
Territoriality
   Legability
Lifecare (lifelease) contracts
Proprietary vs. non-profit facilities
Long-term care
Older Americans Act
Housing Policy
   Section 202
   Section 236
   Section 8
   SRO housing

Topics for Discussion

1. What aspects of person-environment congruence are most important in selecting housing for an older person who must relocate from his own home to a nursing home?

2. Describe the fear-victimization paradox in the elderly, and possible reasons for its existence. What potential solutions exist to alleviate this problem?

3. Discuss some options available to an older person who does not wish to move to retirement housing, but prefers to stay in the large mortgage-free home in which she has lived for 40 years, but which she can no longer maintain.

4. Describe the advantages and disadvantages of the various person-environment models for understanding older people's interactions with their social and physical environment.

5. Provide some guidelines for designing a multilevel facility for older people that would be suitable for a healthy and active 65-year-old, as well as for a frail,   cognitively impaired 85-year-old.

6. Discuss the pros and cons of assisted living facilities as a residence for an older person who has problems with ADLs.

7.   Describe the impact of the loss of SRO housing on problems of homelessness among older Americans.

Multiple Choice

1. The earliest framework for a person-environment perspective on human behavior is provided by the personality theory proposed by:

   - a. Gubrium
   - X b. Murray
   - c. Lawton & Nahemow
   - d. Erikson

2. A person-environment perspective is useful for understanding human behavior because it assumes that:

   - a. human behavior is consistent across settings
   - b. people behave similarly in the same setting
   - X c. behavior varies as a function of personal and environmental characteristics
   - d. behavior cannot be changed by changing the physical environment

3. According to Gubrium's matrix of social contexts, which of the following housing environments will be most likely to encourage friendship formation among residents?

   - a. heterogeneous ages and high proximity
   - X b. homogeneous ages and high proximity
   - c. homogeneous ages and low proximity
   - d. heterogeneous ages and low proximity

4. A model that examines person-environment relations vis-à-vis the older person's competence is that developed by:

   - X a. Lawton & Nahemow
   - b. Kahana
   - c. French, Rodgers & Cobb
   - d. Murray

5. Compared to younger age groups, people over age 65 are _____ likely to move to a different community and _____ likely to change housing types.

   - X a. less/more
   - b. less/less
   - c. more/more
   - d. more/less

6. Institutional relocation need not result in increased rates of mortality and morbidity if:

    a. the new facility fosters greater dependency than the old one
    b. the older person is given a new support system in the new setting
    c. the new facility is newly constructed
X   d. the older person is personally involved in the move

7. Which of the following older groups is <u>least</u> likely to live in central cities?

X   a. Whites
    b. African Americans
    c. Hispanic
    d. all three are evenly distributed

8. Social interaction with young and old neighbors and friends is greatest for older people who live in:

    a. urban settings
    b. high rise apartments
X   c. small communities
    d. suburban tract housing

9. The group that experiences the highest rates of victimization in all categories is the group that is aged:

X   a. 12 to 25
    b. 35 to 55
    c. 65 to 75
    d. 85 and older

10. Fear of crime is highest among older persons who:

    a. live on isolated farms
X   b. live in central cities
    c. own their homes
    d. are economically independent

11. Older people who have lived in their own home for many years and can no longer maintain them:

    a. should move into special housing for elders
    b. will be happiest if they can take in young renters
X   c. are experiencing P-E incongruence
    d. should take a reverse mortgage on their homes

12. Studies of relocation to planned housing by low income older persons have found:

    a.   improved functional health following the move
X b.   increased housing satisfaction
    c.   increased mortality rates
    d.   objectively assessed improvement in psychological adaptation

13. Multilevel housing for older people:

    a.   means that the housing is most likely high rise apartments
    b.   always includes skilled nursing care
    c.   generally requires payment of a founder's fee
X d.   allows movement to higher levels of care as needed

14. The chances of an older American being institutionalized at some time during his/her lifetime are:

    a.   almost 50%
X b.   above 25%
    c.   very low, less than 5%
    d.   we don't really know the chances

15. The majority of nursing homes today:

    a.   are occupied by minority groups
    b.   are non-profit facilities
X c.   are proprietary facilities
    d.   are designed for cognitively impaired elders

16. Studies of privacy needs among various age groups have revealed:

X a.   older people in nursing homes have varying needs for privacy
    b.   older people in nursing homes have less need for privacy than those in the community
    c.   older people in nursing homes have less need for privacy than the young
    d.   relocation to a congregate facility reduces one's need for privacy

17. A disadvantage of assisted living as a long-term care option today is that:

    a.   it can only house well elderly
    b.   it costs more than nursing home care
    c.   health services are not provided
X d.   most states do not provide Medicaid waivers

18.   Studies of homeless men have found that:

      a.   very few are over age 60
X   b.   many who qualify for social services do not get them
      c.   most use medical services regularly
      d.   most are using prescriptions for psychiatric disorders

True or False

1. The person-environment perspective is useful in gerontology because older people's ability to control their environment is often diminished.

   True _X_   False _____

2. Researchers have found that an oversupply of an environmental characteristic vis-à-vis an individual's needs is generally better for maintaining life satisfaction than is an undersupply.

   True _____   False _X_

3. The majority of older people today live in suburbs.

   True _____   False _X_

4. Surveys have revealed a greater proportion of older people who live near their children in urban communities than in rural areas.

   True _X_   False _____

5. The majority of older people live in single family homes that they own.

   True _X_   False _____

6. Public housing for older people should be located near freeways in order to make it easier for them to reach a variety of services.

   True _____   False _X_

7. Congregate housing is better for many older people than private apartments because meals are more likely to be provided for residents on site.

   True _X_   False _____

8. Many national surveys have revealed that fear of crime is a greater concern for many older people than their concerns about income or health status.

   True _X_   False _____

9. The proportion of older persons in nursing homes at any one time is higher in the U.S. than in any other Western country.

    True _____   False _X_

10. The primary factor that appears to determine nursing home placement is the older person's cognitive status.

    True _____   False _X_

11. Medicare currently does not reimburse fully the costs entailed by older people who are placed in adult day centers.

    True _X_   False _____

12. The major source of funding for nursing home residents is Medicare.

    True _____   False _X_

13. Federal and state accessibility codes have established standards that require buildings to be better designed in order to meet the special sensory and physical needs of older residents.

    True _____   False _X_

14. SRO housing is becoming scarcer as an option for low income older people in urban centers.

    True _X_   False _____

15. Assisted living has been shown to be appropriate for only a small proportion of frail elders.

    True _____   False _X_

CHAPTER 14: ECONOMIC STATUS, WORK, AND RETIREMENT

Key Terms

Productive aging
Full and part-time employment
Age Discrimination in Employment Act
Average age of retirement
Retirement as:
    An institution
    A process/transition/role exit/
        "unretirement"
Social Security
    underlying assumptions
    Cost of living adjustment
Displaced homemakers

Pensions
    General public pensions
    Job-specific pensions
    Public employee pensions
    Private pensions
    Vesting and portability
Employment Retirement Income
    Security Act
Percentage of older people who are poor
Gender and ethnic differences in poverty
Near poor or at-risk of poverty ("tweeners")
Supplemental Security Income

Topics for Discussion

1. How are changing demographic, economic and social patterns likely to influence the employment/retirement patterns of men and women in the next 10 to 15 years?

2. If you were the Director of Personnel in a corporation that wanted to maximize older workers' skills, what steps would you recommend to your company (e.g., changes in policies, programs, benefits, etc.)?

3. How would you explain the research findings that most people state that they would prefer to be employed, even though most choose to retire early?

4. What are the primary barriers to the employment of individuals over age 65? What are some strategies to overcome them?

5. In planning for or thinking about your own retirement, what factors do you consider to be most important? What would you like to do upon retirement? What steps can you take now to help you achieve your retirement goals?

6. How would you respond to the argument by some politically conservative organizations that older adults are financially better off than any other age group in our society and are "greedy geezers"?

7.   Discuss the reasons that certain groups of older people are more likely to be living in poverty than others (e.g. groups defined by age, gender, ethnic minority status, living arrangements, type of occupation, etc.).

8.   If you were advocating for reforms in Social Security to reduce income disparities by gender and ethnic minority status, what changes would you suggest? What is your rationale for these changes?

Multiple Choice

1. Patterns of employment since the 1930's suggest that there has been:

       a. an increase in the number of people over age 50 employed full-time
   X b. a trend toward early retirement
       c. a decrease in the number of people over age 50 employed part-time
       d. none of the above

2. Increased longevity and changing employment patterns have resulted in:

   X a. both men and women spending more years in employment
       b. a greater proportion of the life span devoted to paid employment
       c. fewer women entering the work force
       d. women not entering the work force until after childbearing is completed

3. The employment patterns of older workers are more likely than younger workers to be characterized by:

   X a. part-time jobs
       b. low or entry-level positions
       c. high tech positions
       d. all of the above

4. The greatest barriers to <u>part-time</u> employment are:

       a. Social Security limits on the amount that can be earned after age 62
       b. employers resistance to the additional health care costs
       c. employer policies against employees drawing partial pensions
   X d. all of the above
       e. none of the above

5. The apparent contradiction between more older people seeking employment after they have chosen early retirement can be explained by:

       a. economic factors
       b. a desire to feel productive
       c. social needs
   X d. all of the above
       e. none of the above

6. Which of the following will <u>not</u> be a barrier to employment for future cohorts of older people?

   a. age discrimination
X b. mandatory retirement
   c. negative stereotypes
   d. lack of opportunities

7. In the 21st century, the workforce will be characterized by:

X a. more older people seeking employment
   b. more younger workers seeking employment
   c. wide availability of higher paying positions
   d. none of the above

8. Which of the following is a <u>false</u> description of retirement?

   a. Retirement is a social institution.
X b. Retirement is a time of inevitable physical decline and poor health.
   c. Retirement is a process.
   d. Retirement is an opportunity for personal growth and learning new roles.

9. The primary factor(s) that affect when a worker will retire is(are):

   a. the amount of retirement preparation
   b. the type of job
   c. his/her attitude toward leisure
X d. his/her health and retirement income

10. The retirement process for older ethnic minorities can be described as:

    a. similar to white retirees
X   b. blurring of the line between work and nonwork
    c. a time of economic security and good health
    d. none of the above

11. Which of the following factors is most important for good adjustment during retirement?

    a. a person's place of residence
    b. a person's gender
    c. previous occupation
X   d. adequacy of income

12. Since 1986, the mandatory retirement age for most occupations is:

    a. 62
    b. 65
    c. 70
X   d. there is no mandatory retirement

13. Older people who are unemployed and seeking employment must overcome a number of common obstacles. Which of the following is/are frequently encountered?

    a. subtle forms of age discrimination
    b. employers' reluctance to retrain older workers
    c. technological and workplace changes
    d. "rusty" job-hunting techniques
X   e. all of the above

14. A comprehensive approach to retirement planning should include:

    a. financial planning
    b. health promotion
    c. leisure planning
    d. restructuring of work patterns
X   e. all of the above

15. The primary reason for seeking employment after retirement is:

    a. the desire to make a contribution to the community
    b. the desire for the sociability of the job
X   c. the need to supplement retirement income
    d. boredom

16. Which of the following statements is <u>false</u> regarding retirement?

    a. Retirement has been found to be related to mental illness
    b. Retirement has been found to cause an increase in the number of physical health problems experienced.
    c. Most people retire because they have to (i.e. mandatory retirement).
    d. Retirement has been found to be associated with a marked decrease in participation in community organizations.
X   e. all of the above

17. Which of the following is <u>true</u> regarding Social Security?

    a. It provides an adequate retirement income for most retirees.
    b. The Social Security trust funds will go bankrupt in the next 5-10 years.
X   c. It is based upon the concept of earned rights (i.e., benefits in proportion to what a person has paid into the system).
    d. all of the above.
    e. none of the above

18. The largest source of income for older persons is:

    a. savings and other assets
    b. pensions
X   c. Social Security
    d. salary and wages

19. Job-specific private pensions:

    a. cover all retirees of private companies
    b. generally are equivalent to 80% of a retiree's employment income
    c. typically include annual cost of living increases
X   d. are more likely to benefit long-term, middle and upper-income employees.

20. Perceptions of older people as financially better off than any other age group overlook the fact that:

    a. older people are more likely to be among the near-poor than other age groups
    b. there are "hidden poor" among the older population
    c. there are pockets of poverty among women, ethnic minorities, and the oldest-old
X   d. all of the above
    e. none of the above

21. The percentage of older people who fall below the official poverty line is:

    a. approximately 50%
    b. less than 5%
X   c. approximately 12%
    d. approximately 25%

22. Which of the following are characteristics of the Supplemental Security Income (SSI) program?

    a. There are limits on assets and income.
    b. Benefits can be reduced if relatives provide assistance.
    c. More women than men depend on SSI.
    d. The application process is complex.
X   e. all of the above.

23. Among all age groups, the poorest are:

    a. the young old, aged 60-65
    b. all women under the age of 45
X   c. ethnic minority women over age 75
    d. ethnic minority men over age 75

True or False

1. Most people experience retirement as a time of dramatic changes in their leisure activities and interests.

    True _____   False _X_

2. Deterioration in mental or physical health is a primary consequence of retirement.

    True _____   False _X_

3. Mandatory retirement is the major cause of the trend toward early retirement.

    True _____   False _X_

4. Employment studies show that older workers are as productive as younger workers but their absenteeism rate is higher.

    True _____   False _X_

5. Once out of work, workers over age 40 remain unemployed longer and are more likely to become discouraged than younger persons.

    True _X_   False _____

6. Researchers have found that early retirement generally has more negative effects than later retirement, especially for those who do not plan for their retirement.

    True _X_   False _____

7. Marital satisfaction generally increases because of retirement.

    True _____   False _X_

8. The age at which workers can collect full Social Security benefits is 62 years.

    True _____   False _X_

9. The primary source of income in retirement is personal savings.

    True _____   False _X_

10. Older people on Social Security are financially penalized if they are employed and earn over a certain amount set by the federal government.

    True X   False _____

11. Social Security provisions favor the two-career family.

    True _____   False X

12. Homemakers are automatically now covered by Social Security based on their own contribution to the home.

    True _____   False X

13. Fortunately, the majority of older people have benefits from both pensions and Social Security.

    True _____   False X

14. The proportion of men and women over age 65 who are employed in the 1990s is greater than ever before.

    True _____   False X

15. The poverty rate among the older population has decreased since the late 1960s, largely because of benefits from Social Security and Medicare.

    True X   False _____

16. The Social Security trust fund will be bankrupt by the year 2000.

    True _____   False X

17. Eligibility for Supplemental Security Income (SSI) is determined on the basis of number of years worked in covered employment.

    True _____   False X

18. A primary reason for some older adults' low socioeconomic status is that Social Security has not kept pace with inflation.

    True _____   False X

CHAPTER 15: CHANGING ROLES: COMMUNITY, ORGANIZATIONAL, AND POLITICAL

Key Terms

Productive aging
Leisure: variations by gender, class,
     age and ethnic minority status
Voluntary associations
Volunteerism (functions, consequences)
    Foster Grandparents Program
    Senior Companion Program
    Older American Volunteer Program
    Service Corps of Retired Executives
     (SCORE)
    Retired Senior Volunteer Program
Religious participation
    Religiousness
    Spiritual well-being
    Variations by ethnic minority status
Voting behavior

Factors that affect political participation
    Stage in life cycle
    Historical or period effects
    Cohort effects
    Gender, socioeconomic class and
     ethnic minority status
Senior power:
    Subculture theory of aging
    Politics of new aging and diversity
Age-based political power and organizations
    Townsend movement
    McClain movement
    National Council of Senior Citizens
    National Association of Retired Federal
     Employees
    American Association of Retired Persons
    National Council on the Aging
    National Caucus for the Black Aged
    National Hispanic Council on Aging
    National Indian Council on Aging
    Older Women's League
    Gray Panthers

Topics for Discussion

1. Presuming that you were a director of a senior center that depends upon volunteers, what steps would you take to recruit and retain older people as volunteers?

2. Discuss the concept of productive aging. What are ways that older people can continue to play meaningful roles in our society? What are barriers to such roles?

3. Think about how you spend your own leisure time now. What benefits do you derive from your current leisure activities? What kinds of leisure activities would you anticipate participating in when you are older? Would they represent a continuation of or a change from current activities?

4. What is your perspective on the use of volunteers to perform functions that might otherwise be performed by paid staff?

5. What are some of the major challenges facing senior centers in the 1990's? If you were a senior center director, what kinds of programmatic changes would you recommend to your board?

6. What should churches be doing to meet older adults' religious and spiritual needs?

7. From your knowledge of local and national political events, do you perceive the older population as a powerful political constituency? If not, what factors prevent them from exerting the power of their numbers?

8. Discuss the pros and cons of age-based organizations versus intergenerational alliances to influence legislation.

Multiple Choice

1. The concept of productive aging refers to:

    a. paid work
    b. successful aging
X   c. the variety of valuable roles that older people play
    d. none of the above

2. Which of the following functions can be fulfilled by leisure?

    a. For some individuals, leisure can provide a meaningful substitute to the work role.
    b. For some individuals, work-like activities as leisure provide satisfaction.
    c. For some individuals, "keeping busy" is satisfying.
    d. none of the above
X   e. all of the above

3. Leisure patterns in old age tend to:

X   a. be marked by more solitary and sedentary activities
    b. show a departure from leisure activities in earlier years
    c. have little association with feelings of well-being
    d. consist of boring activities

4. Performing routine household chores can serve which of the following functions for an older person?

    a. be a means to maintain competence levels
    b. be a way of coping with environmental changes
    c. be a source of self-esteem
    d. provide personal satisfaction
X   e. all of the above

5. Although senior centers can provide meaningful leisure activities, they do not serve the majority of older people. Reasons for this include:

    a. poor health among many who would benefit
    b. older people's prejudice against participating with other older adults
    c. programs are often perceived as irrelevant to low-income elderly
    d. too few men participate
X   e. all of the above

6. Voluntary association membership appears to be most strongly associated with life satisfaction when:

    a. older people interact with younger people
X   b. older people have significant and influential roles within the voluntary association
    c. older people have numerous opportunities to socialize with younger people
    d. older people have the money to join such associations

7. The social theory which best explains patterns of volunteer activity in old age is:

    a. disengagement
X   b. continuity
    c. person-environment
    d. social exchange

8. Which of the following statements is <u>false</u> about older adults and volunteerism?

    a. Older people who volunteer probably also volunteered when they were younger
X   b. The retirement years are an ideal time to recruit older people as volunteers
    c. Those older adults who volunteer generally derive personal satisfaction from these activities
    d. Some aging advocates maintain that older volunteers should hold more responsible and/or paid positions

9. Rates of volunteering are highest among older people who:

    a. have higher income
    b. are well educated
    c. are married
    d. are satisfied with their lives
X   e. all of the above

10. Which of the following statements about religious participation is <u>true</u>?

    a. Religious participation across the life span peaks in the late 60's or early 70's
    b. Older people engage in fewer internal religious activities (such as reading the Bible) than other age groups
X   c. Religious faith appears to be more influential in older people's lives than in other age groups
    d. Individuals tend to become more religious as they age

11. Research on religiousness is limited by:

X   a. cross-sectional data
     b. longitudinal data
     c. no attention to gender and ethnic minority status
     d. all of the above
     e. none of the above

12. Religious involvement can be an effective coping mechanism and source of social support, particularly for:

     a. those over age 85
X   b. ethnic minority elders
     c. Caucasian women
     d. none of the above

13. Which of the following statements about political participation is false?

     a. In general, older people today vote more conservatively than younger people
X   b. Rates of voting decline sharply with an increase in age
     c. When variables such as education are controlled for, interest in politics increases with age
     d. On some issues, older people vote more liberally than younger people

14. When looking at the political behavior of older people, it is necessary to:

X   a. take account of the historical period in which they were raised
     b. compare the behavior of individuals of various ages at one point in time
     c. take account of their age
     d. try to isolate age differences

15. Instances of low voter turnout among the older population can generally be explained in terms of:

     a. ethnic minority status
     b. gender
     c. education
X   d. all of the above
     e. none of the above

16. The first major attempt by older persons to try to improve their life conditions was called:

    a. the McClain Movement
    b. the Packard-Bell Movement
X   c. the Townsend Movement
    d. the American Association of Retired Persons

17. The argument that older people as a group are politically powerful is based on the assumption that:

    a. older adults have a relatively high ratio of voting and political party membership
    b. there is a growing shared political consciousness among older people
    c. there will be better health and higher education among future older cohorts
X   d. all of the above
    e. none of the above

18. Which of the following statements is advanced by critics of the perspective that older adults are unified and are a significant political force?

    a. The heterogeneity of the older population precludes their sharing an age-based consciousness
    b. Increasingly, older and younger people are forming cross-age alliances
    c. Senior organizations have not had a substantial and long-term impact on social policy, especially for the most disadvantaged groups
    d. Past legislative success has resulted primarily from politicians' beliefs that older adults are worse off and more deserving than other age groups
X   e. all of the above

19. The largest and most influential senior organization is:

    a. National Council of Senior Citizens
    b. Gerontological Society of America
X   c. American Association of Retired Persons
    d. National Council on the Aging

True or False

1. In order to derive satisfaction from life, older people must be involved in active leisure pursuits.

   True _____   False _X_

2. The quality of interactions in leisure pursuits tends to be related to higher life satisfaction and morale than the number and type of leisure pursuits.

   True _X_   False _____

3. The most important factor in determining membership in voluntary associations is age.

   True _____   False _X_

4. Rates of volunteering increase significantly after retirement.

   True _____   False _X_

5. In the past decade, most leisure time has been spent by older adults in public recreation programs designed specifically for them.

   True _____   False _X_

6. People typically become more religious as they grow older.

   True _____   False _X_

7. Religious activities and attitudes have generally been found to be associated with life satisfaction and adjustment to old age.

   True _X_   False _____

8. Spirituality has been found to have little association with life satisfaction and quality of life.

   True _____   False _X_

9. Younger people are more likely to vote in national elections than are the old.

   True _____   False _X_

10. As people age, they generally become more conservative in their voting patterns.

    True _____ False _X_

11. Age is the primary factor in determining how individuals vote on different issues, such as health care and abortion rights.

    True _____   False _X_

12. Most activities by national senior organizations have been oriented to meeting the needs of low-income older individuals.

    True _____   False _X_

13. Educational institutions have taken the lead in developing programs specifically for older adults.

    True _____   False _X_

CHAPTER 16: DEATH, DYING, BEREAVEMENT, AND WIDOWHOOD

Key Terms

Death anxiety
Death fears
Death as an organizer of time
    "Legitimization of biography"
Death as loss
Kubler-Ross: stages of the dying
    process
An appropriate death
Dying trajectory
Dying person's bill of rights
Palliative care
Hospice care

Euthanasia
    Passive (allowing death)
    Active (causing death)
Hemlock Society
Legal options
    Living Will
    Advance directive
    Patient Self-determination Act
    Durable power of attorney
    Guardianship
    Conservatorship
    Choice in dying
    Surrogate decision-making
Bereavement
Anticipatory grief
Mourning
Grief reactions
    Grief work
Gender differences in widowhood

Topics for Discussion

1. What are ways in which our society seeks to deny or avoid death? How do these influence your own attitudes toward death?

2. What are some limitations of Kubler-Ross's stage model of dying? Are you aware of other models about death and dying that address some of these limitations?

3. Discuss ways that psycho-social factors interact with the biological process of dying.

4. What are some issues for people to consider when preparing for death? What can you do in your own life to prepare for your own death?

5. What is your own position on euthanasia? With regard to the elderly? With regard to youth? What would you want for yourself if you were terminally ill? What would you include if you were writing a Living Will?

6. What can human service professionals do to protect the rights of dying patients and to ensure a "good death"? Discuss ways that these goals may be in conflict with one another.

7. Discuss both the ethical and legal issues related to dying in a time period of increased life expectancy and life-prolonging medical techniques.

8. If you were a health care professional working in a nursing home, what kinds of services would you develop to help older residents cope with dying, death and bereavement?

Multiple Choice

1. Cultures develop different views on dying. Which of the following perspectives is true of our society?

   a. Death is viewed as an unnatural event which is to be fought off as long as possible.
   b. Death is viewed primarily as a province of the old.
   c. Death is both denied and accepted.
   d. Some types of rituals such as funerals can ease the mourning process for most survivors

   X e. all of the above

2. Before the twentieth century, death

   X a. generally occurred at home
   b. was a phenomenon largely of old age
   c. was peripheral to younger people's awareness
   d. all of the above

3. Studies of fears of death indicate that:

   a. older adults are morbidly fearful of death
   b. fear of death increases among those with terminal conditions

   X c. older people typically have fewer fears about death than younger people do
   d. most older adults do not think about death very much
   e. none of the above

4. Older adults may fear death less than younger people because:

   a. older adults view their lives as having less future promise and less value
   b. older adults often have a sense of living on "borrowed time"
   c. older adults' experiences with the deaths of relatives and friends can help them anticipate and accept dying
   d. dying later in life is an "on-time" event

   X e. all of the above.

5. Which of the following is <u>not</u> a stage in the dying process, as presented by Kubler-Ross?

   a. denial
   b. anger

   X c. hope
   d. bargaining
   e. acceptance

6. In Kubler-Ross's stages of dying, patients typically:

    a. go through the stages in exact order
    b. finally make it to acceptance
X   c. may move back and forth between stages, and be in several stages at once
    d. do not usually deny their diagnosis

7. The dying trajectory framework recognizes that:

X   a. the dying patient, family members, and helping professionals all perceive a course of dying and an expected time of death.
    b. there is no predictability to the pace of dying.
    c. professionals, family members, and the dying person nearly always agree about the pace of dying.
    d. none of the above

8. Which of the following are common criticisms of Kubler-Ross's theory?

    a. Dying individuals often go through stages in different sequence and may repeat some.
    b. For some people, denial or anger may be a healthier way to face death than acceptance is.
    c. Dying people tend to experience a variety of reactions rather than an orderly progression of stages.
X   d. all of the above
    e. none of the above

9. Hospice care includes:

    a. a philosophy of care for the terminally ill
    b. support for families of dying persons
    c. methods to minimize the pain experienced by the terminally ill
X   d. all of the above
    e. none of the above

10. Increased recognition of the needs of dying patients has led to the development of:

    a. legal and medical debates about the right to die
    b. hospices
    c. counseling programs for the dying and their families
X   d. all of the above
    e. none of the above

11. Proponents of the right to die with dignity would <u>disagree</u> with which of the following statements?

X   a. Most older people should die in a hospital to ensure the best care.
      b. Doctors know more about treating illness than about when not to provide treatment.
      c. The high cost of dying is burdening the health care system.
      d. Helping an older person obtain a good death is a desirable goal.

12. We would <u>not</u> expect the process of life review to include:

      a. increased awareness of experiences
X   b. increased fear and anxiety
      c. preparation for one's own death
      d. increased significance and meaning to life
      e. reconciliation with estranged relatives or friends

13. The general public's attitude toward the "right to die" is that:

      a. it is immoral.
      b. active euthanasia is best.
X   c. people of all ages should have the right to refuse treatment.
      d. only older adults should have the right to refuse treatment.

14. Suspending all available interventions, including feeding, in order to relieve suffering is called:

X   a. passive euthanasia
      b. active euthanasia
      c. mercy killing
      d. all of the above

15. Taking actions deliberately to shorten a person's life, such as providing a lethal injection, in order to end suffering is called:

      a. passive euthanasia
      b. voluntary elective death
X   c. active euthanasia
      d. failure to care

16. Assisted suicide is characterized by all the following <u>except</u> for

    a. another person provides the means by which an individual ends his or her life
X   b. it has become legal in several states as a result of the Kevorkian cases.
    c. it is supported by the Hemlock Society
    d. public support for it is growing

17. A Living Will is a document that states:

    a. the terms of the writer's estate
    b. the writer's religious belief
X   c. what medical action, if any, should be taken if the writer becomes mentally incompetent or terminally ill
    d. all of the above
    e. none of the above

18. A durable power of attorney:

    a. applies only to the terminally ill
    b. is a substitute for a living will
X   c. appoints another person to make decisions in the event the writer becomes incompetent
    d. all of the above

19. A legal document that establishes control over an individual's person, property and finances is called a:

    a. conservatorship
    b. Living Will
X   c. guardianship
    d. durable power of attorney

20. Don's wife is terminally ill, and he has begun to grieve. This is called _____ grief.

    a. preparatory
    b. premature
    c. inappropriate
X   d. anticipatory

21. Which of the following stages do <u>not</u> typically occur in the grief reaction to death?

    a. shock, numbness, and disbelief
    b. idealization of the loved one who has died
    c. reorganization
X   d. hope

22. In working with relatives regarding their grief, health care providers must:

X   a. be sensitive to cultural and ethnic differences regarding death
     b. discourage relatives from spending money on a funeral
     c. help move them quickly to the acceptance phase of grief
     d. all of the above

23. Older widows may find widowhood to be more difficult than older widowers do because:

X   a. they are more likely to face financial hardships than widowers.
     b. they have fewer friends to turn to than widowers do.
     c. they move in with adult children shortly after their spouse's death.
     d. they are more lonely than widowers are.
     e. they have more difficulty expressing their grief than widowers do.

24. Women become widows at the average age of:

     a. 72
     b. 60
X   c. 56
     d. 45

25. Women who cope best with widowhood seem to be those who:

     a. see their children frequently
X   b. have a network of friends
     c. were widowed early in life
     d. all of the above

26. The death of a spouse may be one of the most stressful events that an older person will experience because:

     a. typically, it negatively affects the surviving spouse's health.
     b. for most people, it leads to long-term difficulties in coping.
     c. depression, loneliness and sadness become chronic.
     d. all of the above
X   e. none of the above

TRUE OR FALSE

1. One of the major assumptions of Kubler-Ross's work is that dying can be a time of growth and meaning.

   True _X_   False _____

2. Kubler-Ross's stages of dying appear to be universal.

   True _X_   False _____

3. Death as an organizer of time refers to the belief held by many older people that they can accomplish little of meaning in the remaining time.

   True _X_   False _____

4. An appropriate death means that a person has died at home surrounded by loved ones.

   True _____   False _X_

5. Psychotherapy is of limited personal value to older dying patients.

   True _____   False _X_

6. Natural death legislation permits relatives to actively aid a dying person in ending their life.

   True _____   False _X_

7. An example of passive euthanasia is deliberately giving a lethal injection to end a patient's suffering.

   True _____   False _X_

8. Withholding or withdrawing useless or unwanted medical treatments for patients close to death is both illegal and unethical.

   True _____   False _X_

9. Public and professional acceptance of euthanasia is decreasing.

   True _____   False _X_

10. Younger widows generally find the death of a husband to be more stressful than older widows do, especially in the early stages of grief.

   True _X_   False _____

11. Grief is always less when death is not sudden and the survivors have been able to anticipate it and prepare for changes.

   True _____   False _X_

12. The major problem faced by both widowers and widows is loneliness.

   True _X_   False _____

13. Widow support groups recognize the value of informal help from people who have had similar experiences.

   True _X_   False _____

14. About half of American women become widows around age 56.

   True _X_   False _____

15. Women are more likely than men to remarry after the death of a spouse.

   True _____   False _X_

16. Most survivors successfully resolve their grief within a year.

   True _____   False _X_

CHAPTER 17: POPULATIONS AT RISK: OLDER ETHNIC MINORITIES

Key Terms

Ethnicity: components and functions
Ethnic minorities
Ethnogerontology
Double jeopardy hypothesis
Multiple hierarchy stratification perspective
Racial crossover in life expectancy
Health, income and family characteristics of African American,
   Hispanic American, American Indian and Pacific Asian Elders
Preferential considerations in service delivery
Differential considerations in service delivery

Topics for Discussion

1. What are the major problems facing ethnic minority elders in our society? What do you perceive to be some solutions to these problems? Barriers to these solutions?

2. Apply social exchange theory to an analysis of the status of ethnic minority elders in our society. Cite examples that illustrate the centrality of control over valued resources to their status.

3. Older persons are not a homogeneous population. Identify dimensions along which ethnic minority elders differ from and are similar to the older population in general. Drawing upon your own discipline's research and practice perspective, what are some implications of these dimensions for both research and the delivery of services?

4. Suggest directions for future research on ethnic minority elders. What are some of the difficulties of conducting such research?

5. Describe your own ethnic and cultural experiences and how those might affect your own aging process and that of other members of your family.

6. If you were designing a multicultural senior center (for example, nutrition, health care, recreational activities, and so on), describe typical programs, how they would differ from more traditional centers, and from programs for a specific ethnic group.

7. Describe your own perceptions of the older population of a specific ethnic minority group. To what extent are these stereotypes? To what extent are these based on personal experiences? Do you have any research support for your perceptions?

Multiple Choice

1. Which of the following characteristics is generally associated with ethnic minority status?

   a. lifetime experience with discrimination
   b. formation of a subculture
   c. development of coping structures
X d. all of the above

2. The double jeopardy hypothesis, as first advanced by Tally and Kaplan, suggests that:

   a. With age, differences in income, health and life expectancy diminish.
   b. Women face more disadvantages than men as they age.
X c. Lifetime factors of economic and racial discrimination make it more difficult for ethnic minorities to adjust to old age than for whites.
   d. none of the above

3. All ethnic minority populations share the following characteristic:

   a. The young outnumber the old.
   b. Their median age is lower than for the white population.
   c. They face more economic and health problems than the white population does.
X d. all of the above.

4. Compared with the American older population generally, elders in minority groups are:

   a. more likely to lack access to adequate health care
   b. more likely to have chronic illness
   c. more likely to be poor
   d. less likely to be in a nursing home
X e. all of the above.

5. The poverty of most ethnic minority elders tends to reflect which of the following conditions?

   a. lifelong patterns of unemployment and underemployment
   b. employment in jobs not covered by Social Security
   c. employment in jobs not covered by private pensions
   d. intermittent periods of employment
X e. all of the above.

6.   The ethnic minority population that forms the smallest percentage of the total population age 65 and over is:

a.   African Americans
b.   Pacific Asians
X c.   American Indians
d.   Hispanic Americans

7.   Which of the following statements describing the African American elders is true?

a.   They have a lower prevalence of chronic diseases than whites.
b.   There are proportionately more African American elders in nursing homes compared to whites.
c.   They receive a greater percentage of Social Security benefits than whites.
X d.   After age 85, they become "better survivors."

8.   Which of the following statements describing African American elders is false?

a.   They are poorer than whites.
b.   They are not as healthy as whites.
X c.   Their life expectancy is as long as whites.
d.   They are less well educated than whites.

9.   The African American extended family is generally characterized by:

a.   older female family members frequently caring for young children
b.   shared living arrangements because of economic necessity
c.   adult children frequently providing care for older family members
X d.   all of the above

10.   A major source of social and emotional support for African Americans, outside of family is

a.   the federal government
b.   senior centers
X c.   the church
d.   self-help groups
e.   none of the above

11.   Which of the following statements regarding Hispanic American elders is true?

     a. The majority live in rural areas.
X   b. They are composed of several different subgroups, each with a distinct national/cultural heritage.
     c. They use health services proportionately more than whites and other ethnic minorities.
     d. Their median age is significantly higher than whites and other ethnic minorities.

12.   A major reason that some Hispanics do not seek out social services is:

     a. their relatives provide all the assistance they need.
X   b. they may have been illegal immigrants.
     c. they do not want assistance.
     d. they expect the service system to seek them out.

13.   Among Hispanic families, older members have traditionally:

     a. played only a minor role in child-rearing
     b. been ignored by younger members
X   c. received a great deal of respect and community support
     d. had little influence in family decision-making
     e. both a and d

14.   Which of the following statements about American Indian elders is true?

     a. The Bureau of Indian Affairs has supported the traditional roles of American Indian elders.
X   b. Diseases such as TB, cirrhosis of the liver, and diabetes are common.
     c. They are frequent users of public social and health services.
     d. A small percentage live with other family members.

15.   Pacific Asian elders have long been neglected because:

     a. they have so few problems.
X   b. it is assumed that they will take care of their own.
     c. they are primarily women.
     d. they are financially better off than other ethnic minority groups.

16.   Pacific Asian elders differ from other ethnic minority groups in that:

     a. they are primarily third generation.
     b. there are proportionately more women than in other ethnic groups.
X   c. there are proportionately more men than in other ethnic groups.
     d. they underutilize social and health services.

127

17. Which of the following statements about Pacific Asian elders is <u>false</u>?

    a. Pacific Asians who immigrated to the U.S. before 1924 are less educated, less likely to speak English, and more economically disadvantaged than are other Pacific Asians.
X b. They are high utilizers of medical services and hospital care.
    c. More Pacific Asian elders live below the poverty line than their white counterparts.
    d. They often fail to apply for public assistance programs for which they are qualified.

18. The least amount of data is available about:

    a. African American elders
    b. Hispanic American elders
X c. American Indian elders
    d. Pacific Asian elders

19. Which of the following factors would <u>not</u> serve to increase the utilization of social and health services by older ethnic minorities?

    a. increased numbers of bilingual staff
    b. services that build upon and respect cultural values and community strengths
X c. centralized services so that all ethnic minorities could utilize one focal point for services
    d. transportation provided to services

20. In developing health and long-term care for ethnic minority elders, it is important to:

    a. be sensitive to the utilization of folk medicine and healing
    b. formulate an holistic and wellness-oriented approach
    c. utilize the informal supports of family, friends and community
X d. all of the above
    e. none of the above

True or False

1. Ethnicity refers to minority status within our society.

   True _____   False _X_

2. For all ethnic minority populations, a proportionately higher percentage of older members are in nursing homes than for their white counterparts.

   True _____   False _X_

3. The <u>racial minority crossover</u> phenomenon refers to findings that the death rate for African Americans age 85 and over is lower than for whites age 85 and over.

   True _X_   False _____

4. African American elders tend to be highly dissatisfied with their lives.

   True _____   False _X_

5. The primary factor underlying the relative youthfulness of the Hispanic American population is its high mortality rate.

   True _____   False _X_

6. Compared to other groups of older adults, American Indian elders tend to turn more to governmental programs for support.

   True _____   False _X_

7. Chronological age is the most accurate way to identify the need for services among older American Indians.

   True _____   False _X_

8. Compared to other groups of older adults, Pacific Asian elders are more likely to live in extended family arrangements.

   True _X_   False _____

9. The primary factor underlying the underutilization of social and health services by all ethnic minority groups is strong family support systems which can take care of their older relatives.

   True _____   False _X_

10.   Of all older people, African Americans are the least likely to enter a nursing home.

       True _X_   False _____

11.   There is widespread agreement among service providers about the need for preferential
       services targeted to ethnic minorities, regardless of their level of need.

       True _____   False _X_

CHAPTER 18: POPULATIONS AT RISK: OLDER WOMEN

Key Terms

Interaction of gender and age
Feminization of poverty
Employment patterns
Most frequent chronic illnesses and effects
Osteoporosis
Marital status and gender differences
Earnings sharing in Social Security
Older Women's League

Topics for Discussion

1. Compare the changing status of men and women in old age. What are some of the reasons for gender-related differences in old age?

2. How can you explain the fact that women live longer than men but are less healthy than their male counterparts in old age?

3. In designing policies and programs for older women, what are factors about their socialization experiences that you would need to consider? How would you try to address these?

4. What do you view to be the major problems facing older women in our culture? From the perspective of your discipline, what are two strategies toward solving the problems facing older women?

5. What do you perceive to be the major strengths/resources controlled by older women? From a policy or program perspective, what would be strategies for building upon these strengths?

6. What types of policy changes are needed to address the economic problems faced by older women?

Multiple Choice

1. The primary reason that older women have become a special focus of some gerontological research is:

    a. they form the fastest growing segment of our population.
    b. they are more likely to face social problems than older men are.
    c. they live longer than men.
    X d. all of the above

2. The greatest problem faced by older women today is:

    a. osteoporosis
    b. menopause
    X c. inadequate income
    d. mental illness

3. The percentage of older women living in poverty is:

    a. over 70%
    b. less than 10%
    X c. approximately 16%
    d. approximately 33%

4. Among older women, the increase in the poverty rate is <u>greatest</u> among:

    X a. ethnic minority women
    b. unmarried women living alone
    c. the frail (e.g., age 75 and over)
    d. none of the above
    e. all of the above

5. There is a saying that "women are only one man away from poverty." Why would that be true?

    a. Homemakers are not eligible for Social Security
    b. If a women works, she is often paid less than a man in the same position.
    c. If a women works, she is often employed in a field that pays less than fields that men typically go into.
    d. Their jobs typically do not include pension benefits
    X e. all of the above

6. Status characteristics associated with poverty in old age are:

    a. gender
    b. ethnic minority status
    c. age
    d. living alone
X e. all of the above

7. Women's retirement income is generally characterized by which of the following?

    a. They usually collect full Social Security benefits.
    b. They generally collect Social Security benefits on the basis of their own employment history.
X c. They are more likely than their male counterparts to collect only the minimum Social Security benefits.
    d. They typically enjoy the combined income of Social Security and private pensions.

8. Social Security affects older women in which of the following ways?

    a. Women's benefits tend to be lower than men's.
    b. Widows with survivors' benefits generally receive lower benefits than retired workers do.
    c. Women who are divorced before ten years of marriage are not entitled to any of their former husband's benefits.
    d. A homemaker receives no Social Security credit for her work.
X e. all of the above

9. Older women's participation in private pension systems has been characterized by the fact that:

    a. most women get by financially on survivors' benefits selected by their husbands.
X b. pension systems reward the long-term steady worker with high earnings and job stability.
    c. divorced women can still enjoy their former husbands' pension benefit.
    d. pension provisions enacted by Congress in 1980 will fortunately benefit this current cohort of retired women.

10. Compared to their male counterparts, older women's health status is characterized as follows:

    a. they are healthier.
X b. they are less likely to face life-threatening, high-risk conditions.
    c. they experience fewer days of restricted activity and disability.
    d. they are less likely to take curative action when they are ill.

11. The major reason that older women have less access to group health insurance of their own is:

    a. women are not as healthy as men.
    b. women visit doctors more often than men.
X c. women are less likely to be employed or are only sporadically employed.
    d. women can rely upon their husbands' insurance.
    e. women can depend on Medicare to cover their health care costs.

12. A primary reason that women age 75 and over are more likely to be institutionalized than older men is:

    a. they are not as healthy as their male counterparts age 75 and over.
    b. they are iess likely to be married.
    c. they have fewer available resources for home-based care.
    d. they are likely to have outlived some of their children.
X e. all of the above

13. Which of the following statements is <u>false</u> when describing the social status of older women?

    a. Older women have fewer chances to remarry than their male counterparts.
X b. Older women have fewer close friends than older men.
    c. Older women are more likely to be widowed than older men.
    d. Older women living alone have been found to be most at risk for needing social and health services.
    e. Older women are more likely to rely on adult children for support than on their husbands.

14. Among all age groups, the poorest are:

    a. the young old, aged 60-65
    b. all women under the age of 45
X c. ethnic minority women over age 75
    d. ethnic minority men over age 75
    e. none of the above

True or False

1. Because they comprise the majority of the older population, old women have long been the focus of gerontological research.

   True _____   False _X_

2. A primary reason for older women's economic vulnerability is that most women did not work consistently for pay.

   True _X_   False _____

3. If earnings sharing were implemented as part of Social Security, each partner in marriage would have a separate Social Security account, regardless of their employment status.

   True _X_   False _____

4. Osteoporosis is especially problematic because of the associated risk of bone fractures.

   True _X_   False _____

5. The majority of older women live with husbands or other family members.

   True _____   False _X_

6. Eighty-five percent of women outlive their husbands.

   True _X_   False _____

7. Compared to men, women have more social resources to draw upon in old age.

   True _X_   False _____

8. The Older Women's League is a political interest group open only to women age 65 and over.

   True _____   False _X_

9. Fortunately, the economic status of old women in the future will be substanially improved over the current cohort.

   True _____   False _X_

CHAPTER 19: SOCIAL POLICIES TO ADDRESS SOCIAL PROBLEMS

Key Terms

Social policy and programs
"Graying of the federal budget"
Eligibility criteria
Entitlement funds
    Age entitlement
    Need entitlement
    Form of benefits
    Universal or selective
        Direct or indirect
        Cash transfer/ substitute
Methods of financing
    Contributory or noncontributory
Social construction of social problems
Factors affecting the development of
    policies
    Cultural values
    Public attitudes
    Public perceptions of older
        people
Categorical, residual and incremental
    policies
"Modern aging" period
    "Compassionate" stereotypes
    "Service enterprise"
    "Blaming the victim" or scapegoating
        older people

Social Security: Social adequacy and individual
    equity
Supplemental Security Income
Private pensions
Tax benefits
Title XX or the Social Services Block Grant
Older Americans Act
The Aging Services Network
        Area agencies on aging
        State units on aging
        The aging enterprise
Intergenerational inequity vs. interdependence
    of generations framework
Generational investment
        The "politics of entitlement"
        Concord Coalition
The "politics of productivity"
The "New Aging" and the "politics of diversity"
Public/private division of responsibility
Decentralization of services

Topics for Discussion

1. What factors underlie the relatively slow development of social policy for older adults in the United States, and the incremental, residual nature of the policies that have been formulated? How does this contrast with other Western industrialized societies?

2. Identify the pros and cons of age-based verses needs-based services. Which approach -- or combination of approaches -- do you support and why?

3. What do you perceive to be some limitations/gaps of the current Social Security system? What is your position on the advantages and disadvantages of instituting a means test for Social Security?

4. Debate the arguments expressed by the intergenerational inequity proponents and those of the interdependence of generations perspective. What are the strengths and limitations of each argument? Where do you stand in terms of these arguments? What is the evidence to support your position?

5. What is your perspective on the appropriate division of responsibility between the public and private sectors in addressing problems facing older people?

6. What are the primary ways that the social policies of the "New Aging" in the post-1990's will differ from current public policies?

7. Identify one major societal change that you view as necessary to improve the quality of older persons' lives. What are the barriers to this change? What would be a strategy to bring about the needed change?

Multiple Choice

1. Programs for the older population have been slow to develop in the U.S. because:

     a. our current older population is so small.
     b. families have traditionally cared for their older relatives.
   X c. our culture places a high value on independence and self-reliance.
     d. our older population has not needed assistance until recently.

2. The development of policies for the older adults has benefited from:

     a. our cultural value on individual responsibility
   X b. public perceptions of older people as more deserving than other age groups
     c. the fiscal conservatism of the 1980's
     d. the government's long-range planning capabilities

3. Estes' critique of the manner in which social policies for older adults have developed in our society is that:

     a. human service professionals have benefited more than low-income elders.
     b. older people are defined as a social problem rather than looking at underlying structural causes of problems.
     c. the solution to the problems faced by older people tends to be to provide medical services.
     d. older people are perceived as different from other age groups, therefore requiring separate services
   X e. all of the above

4. Most policies that benefit the older population are:

     a. categorical (age-based) and means-tested
   X b. categorical and universal for all older people
     c. direct cash transfers on the basis of mean-tests
     d. noncontributory and categorical

5. The Social Security System is characterized by:

     a. universal eligibility for all persons
     b. ensuring sufficient retirement income
   X c. providing a minimum floor of protection
     d. all of the above

6.   Which of the following factors affects the revenues available in the Social Security trust fund?

       a. levels of unemployment
       b. changes in the age of eligibility for Social Security benefits
       c. the changing dependency ratios
X   d. all of the above
       e. none of the above

7.   The percent of the federal budget spent on social services and entitlements to older adults is approximately:

       a. 10%
X   b. 30%
       c. 50%
       d. none of the above

8.   A major negative consequence of Title XX (Social Services Block Grant) funding is that:

X   a. low income elders generally compete with other poor groups for resources.b.it provides for only financial support, not other types of assistance.
       c. income is the only criterion for eligibility.
       d. dependent children are excluded from funding.

9.   The agency responsible for administering the programs and services of the Older Americans Act is:

       a. the Social Security Division
X   b. the Administration on Aging
       c. the Federal Council on Aging
       d. the Leadership Council on Aging

10.   Which of the following is not part of the Older American's Act?

       a. the Administration on Aging
       b. state units on aging
X   c. State Association of Nursing Homes
       d. area agencies on aging

11. The primary source of funds of social services specifically for older people is:

    a. Medicare and Medicaid
    b. Social Security
    c. Supplemental Security Income
X d. the Older American's Act and Title XX

12. The perspective that services should be determined on the basis of need, not age, maintains that:

    a. Age is an arbitrary criterion for service delivery.
    b. Age-based criteria stigmatize the older adult.
    c. Age-based criteria assume that older people are different from other age groups.
    d. old age alone is not sufficient grounds for public benefits
X e. all of the above

13. Which of the following viewpoints is not advanced by supporters of the intergenerational inequity perspective?

    a. Younger people will not receive fair returns for their Social Security investments.
X b. Older and younger people have both been hard hit by inflation.
    c. Older adults are draining the federal budget.
    d. Children are poorer than older people are.

14. A basic assumption of the interdependence of generations framework is that:

    a. older adults are financially better off than other age groups.
X b. the family is a major mechanism for intergenerational transfers.
    c. the younger generation only benefits from Social Security when they live long enough to retire.
    d. our society needs to achieve equity or fairness between generations.

15. Since the late 1980's, policy development for the older population has been affected by:

    a. perceptions of the older population as "greedy geezers"
    b. the growing federal deficit
    c. the increasing socioeconomic diversity of the older population
    d. a weak economy
X e. all of the above

16. The "politics of productivity" differ from the "politics of entitlement" in the following ways:

   a. resources are provided on the basis of age.
   b. older adults are viewed as more worthy than other age groups.
X c. older adults are viewed as a resource, providing intergenerational assistance.
   d. all of the above
   e. none of the above

17. Which of the following does not characterize the politics of the "New Aging"?

   a. an intergenerational perspective
   b. the diversity of the older population
X c. an age-based perspective on services
   d. a concern for future generations
   e. none of the above

18. The following trend of concern to many policy makers and groups, such as the Concord Coalition:

   a. the growth of entitlement programs
   b. the rapid growth of programs that benefit primarily older people
   c. the prediction that Medicare trust funds will be depleted shortly after the turn of the century
   d. the perception that the older population is benefiting at the expense of younger people
X e. all of the above

19. Citizen advocacy groups that are organized to advance public policy in the late 1990s are likely to be characterized by:

   a. cultural homogeneity
   b. age homogeneity
X c. alliances that cross cut age, gender and ethnic minority status
   d. political homogeneity
   e. none of the above

20. All of the following are fundamental to the Social Security system except for:

   a. the concept of social insurance
X b, means-testing
   c. universal eligibility
   d. entitlement

True or False

1. The time period in which most of the policies and programs for older people have developed was during the 1980's.

   True _____   False _X_

2. The growing federal and state allocations to programs for older adults have served to create a comprehensive and coordinated system of services.

   True _____   False _X_

3. Social policies for older people tend to be residual and incremental in nature.

   True _X_   False _____

4. The "compassionate" stereotype of older adults as more deserving than other age groups strongly influences current policy developments.

   True _____   False _X_

5. Eligibility for most policies and programs for older people is determined on the basis of income (e.g., means-testing).

   True _____   False _X_

6. Social Security and Medicare have been the primary causes of the growing federal deficit.

   True _____   False _X_

7. The primary cause of the Social Security crisis in the early 1980's was the rapid growth of the older population.

   True _____   False _X_

8. Tax benefits are an example of a policy that serves to benefit nearly all older people.

   True _____   False _X_

9. In the 1980's, children have been the primary beneficiaries of the Social Services Block Grant funding.

   True _X_   False _____

10. Decentralization of services has had numerous benefits for the older population.

   True _____   False _X_

11. The politics of the "New Aging" includes new alliances across age groups on the basis of common needs.

   True _X_   False _____

12. The growing federal and state allocations to programs for older adults have served to create a comprehensive and coordinated system of services accessible to older individuals.

   True _____   False _X_

13. Policy-making in the 1990s can be characterized as a process oriented to advancing efficiency and cost containment.

   True _X_   False _____

14. Recommendations from the Fourth White House Conference on Aging in 1995 emphasized curtailing Medicare and the Older Americans Act.

   True _____   False _X_

CHAPTER 20: HEALTH AND LONG-TERM CARE POLICY AND PROGRAMS

Key Terms

Medicare
   Acute care
   Hospital Insurance (Part A)
   Supplemental Medical
      Insurance (Part B)
   Allowable charges
   Fee-for services system
   Physician "assignment"
   Prospective Payment System (PPS)
   Diagnostic Related Groupings (DRGs)
   Medicare Catastrophic Health Care Act
Medicaid
   "Spend-down" requirement
   Omnibus Budget Reconciliation Act
   Waivers for home and community-based care

Social Services Block Grant
Older Americans Act
Home and community-based care:
   needs and gaps
Private Insurance
   "Medigap" insurance
   Co-payments
National Health Care Reform
   Pepper Commission
   National Health Security Act
Health Maintenance Organizations
Social Health Maintenance
   Organizations
Long-term care in different settings

Topics for Discussion

1. The general public increasingly is concerned about the "crisis in health care," and policy-makers oftentimes blame the rapid growth of the older population for escalating costs in health and long-term care. What do you perceive to be the primary causes for these increasing costs? How would you respond to current arguments that Medicare and Medicaid must be cut and consequently that services to older people must be limited?

2. Describe the ways that long-term care services are organized and funded. What are the underlying assumptions and the consequences of these arrangements?

3. What kinds of changes, if any, would you recommend in Medicare? In this discussion, consider the consequences of changes in Medicare, such as DRGs and increased co-payments.

4. What kinds of changes, if any, would you recommend in Medicaid?

5. Presume that you are testifying before Congress on the need for health care reform. What would be the major components of your proposed reform with regard to older people?

6. Describe the limitations of the growing number of private long-term care insurance schemes from the point of view of older people.

Multiple Choice

1. Medicare is designed to serve:

   a. low-income older adults
   b. institutionalized persons
   c. older people with chronic disabilities
   X d. all persons age 65 and over

2. The biggest problem with current health care systems relative to older people is:

   a. they are oriented toward chronic conditions.
   b. they are oriented toward home care.
   c. they are oriented toward custodial care.
   X d. they are oriented toward acute illness and crisis conditions.
   e. none of the above

3. Which of the following is true of Medicaid?

   a. It provides coverage for a limited amount of health services.
   b. It offers basic hospital and optional supplementary insurance.
   X c. It finances medical care primarily for low-income people who are receiving public assistance or SSI.
   d. It covers medical care costs for people 65 years of age and older as well as for disabled Social Security beneficiaries.
   e. none of the above

4. Nursing home care is primarily financed by:

   a. Supplemental Security Income
   b. personal savings
   X c. Medicaid
   d. Medicare
   e. none of the above

5. In 1965, the new federal legislation establishing Medicare and Medicaid benefits signaled a philosophical change in the U.S. This new philosophy was:

   a. that the federal government should establish a social welfare state
   b. that families should assume the major financial responsibility for their older members
   X c. that our society as a whole has a responsibility to provide health care for the elderly
   d. none of the above

6. The primary factor underlying escalating health and long-term care costs is:

    a. more people reaching old age
    b. older people and their families are paying less for care
    c. older people's disproportionate utilization of health services
 X d. inflation in hospital costs and physicians' fees

7. Medicare covers the following health care costs:

    a. the full amount charged by health care providers
    b. prescription drugs
    c. dental care
    d. hearing and eye exams
 X e. none of the above

8. In an effort to control Medicare costs, the federal government has:

    a. offered incentives for preventive health care
 X b. instituted co-payments and diagnostic related groupings
    c. substantially increased the monthly premiums required for Part B
    d. attempted to change systems of third-party private insurance payments
    e. all of the above

9. The problems of escalating health and long-term care costs will, in the long run, best be solved by:

    a. changing Medicare procedures and regulations
    b. providing catastrophic health insurance for hospital care
 X c. developing a publicly guaranteed, universally available health insurance
    d. limiting the medical interventions available to older people

10. Medicaid public expenditures have grown more rapidly than the federal inflation rate because:

    a. Medicaid funds are administered by states
    b. there has been a rapid increase in the number of Medicaid recipients
    c. Medicaid recipients disproportionately utilize costly health services
 X d. there have been substantial price increases charged by health care providers
    e. all of the above

11. Older people may be reluctant to apply for Medicaid because:

  a. it can carry the stigma of welfare
  b. some physicians are unwilling to treat Medicaid recipients
  c. they will have fewer nursing home options open to them
  d. they must first exhaust their own resources on medical expenses
X e. all of the above

12. Which of the following statements is <u>true</u> about the existing long-term care system?
  a. It provides an adequate and comprehensive system of both community-based and institutional options.
  b. It finances home health care as a way to keep older people in their homes.
X c. It is dominated by institutional care.
  d. It is guided by a national policy on long-term care.

13. A comprehensive system of long-term care should include:

  a. health promotion and prevention of disease
  b. respite and day care
  c. home health care
  d. institutional care and congregate care
X e. all of the above

14. The need for publicly-funded home care services for older people is growing, because:

  a. most older people prefer home care over hospital or nursing home care
  b. Medicare limits the types and amount of "medically necessary" home care that can be reimbursed
  c. growing numbers of older people require non-medical services
X d. all of the above
  e. none of the above

15. Medicaid can be characterized by which of the following:

  a. uniformity of benefits administered federally
X b. coverage of both skilled care for rehabilitation and for intermediate/custodial care in nursing homes
  c. adequate coverage of home and community-based services
  d. all of the above

16. As a whole, health and long-term care services for older people can be characterized by:

    a. the growth of private insurance schemes that adequately fill the gaps left by public funding
X b. growing inequities and the creation of a two tier system of care
    c. increasing emphasis upon the quality of care in hospitals and nursing homes
    d. none of the above

17. The greatest barriers to national health care reform are:

    a. American cultural values on universal access
X b. the resistance of insurance companies and businesses
    c. the unwillingness of physicians to change
    d. none of the above

True or False

1. Family caregivers of older adults most need increased Medicare/Medicaid funding for acute/short-term care.

   True _____   False _X_

2. Fee-for-service is a current health care reimbursement system whereby fees are determined solely on the basis of diagnostic categories.

   True _____   False _X_

3. Medicare is given on the basis of age while Medicaid is given on the basis of financial need.

   True _X_   False _____

4. Long-term care refers specifically to nursing home care.

   True _____   False _X_

5. The higher expenditures for health care for older people are due primarily to older people's more frequent visits to doctors' offices.

   True _____   False _X_

6. Medicare and Medicaid are the fastest growing programs in the federal budget.

   True _X_   False _____

7. The establishment of Medicare has meant that older adults have lower out-of-pocket expenses for health care than they did before the passage of Medicare.

   True _____   False _X_

8. A consequence of the diagnostic related groups (DRGs) is that Medicare patients may be prematurely discharged from hospitals.

   True _X_   False _____

9. Older people are the primary users of Medicaid.

   True _____   False _X_

149

10. Because of the stigma of Medicaid, most older nursing home residents are private pay patients.

    True _____   False _X_

11. Private long-term care insurance is a recent development consistent with the philosophical assumptions underlying Medicare and Medicaid.

    True _____   False _X_

12. Changes in the prospective payment system have service to reduce Medicare costs.

    True _____   False _X_

13. The greatest gap in federal funding for long-term care is home and community-based care.

    True _X_   False _____

14. The proportion of income spent on health care decreases among the lower income older population.

    True _____   False _X_

15. The Social Services Block Grants and the Older Americans Act are able to cover most of the gaps in services left unfunded by Medicare and Medicaid.

    True _____   False _X_

16. President Clinton's proposed health care reform (the National Health Security Act) failed to include coverage for home and community-based services.

    True _____   False _X_

EPILOGUE

Key Terms

Social economic and demographic trends
Multigenerational families
Intergenerational relationships
   Vertical "beanpole" relationships
   Age-condensed family
   Truncated family
   "Women in the middle"
   Reconstituted families
Work-retirement continuum
   Cyclic life plans
   Movement in and out of work
     force
   "Third age"
   Transitions to retirement
   Phased retirement
   Workplace modification
   Job retraining

Productive aging
Successful aging
Integrating leisure across life
   span
Integrating technology into
   homes and caregiving
Long-term care
   Managed care
   Health maintenance
     organizations
Quality vs quantity of life

Topics for Discussion

1. Discuss some potential outcomes of increased longevity with regard to family interactions and obligations. In what ways will changing attitudes toward divorce, remarriage, and women in the work force affect these relationships?

2. Describe current patterns of retirement and how these may change with trends toward re-employment and retraining in some jobs.

3. Discuss some technological advances that will aid older people in the future to live more independently. What are some of the limitations of these advances for older people?

4. In what ways have hospitals and other health care settings begun to address the special needs of older patients? What other steps must acute care settings take to serve this growing population? What are barriers to these changes?

5. Describe the implications of increasing medical technology for bioethical issues related to the treatment of terminally ill older patients.

6. Assuming that you are a gerontologist employed at a local senior center, what programs and activities would you develop to enhance productive aging?

Multiple Choice

1. Demographic trends of the future suggest that people who are over age 65 in the 21st century:

    a. will comprise the majority of the population
    b. will be less educated than the current cohort of older adults
    X c. will have proportionately fewer young to take care of them
    d. will be more likely to rely on federal financial assistance

2. Increased opportunities for ethnic minorities and women today will result in:

    a. equality in earnings between white men and these other groups
    b. a greater proportion of ethnic minorities than whites among the future older population
    c. equal likelihood to suffer from cancer and heart disease as white men
    X d. slight improvements in the economic status of women and ethnic minorities

3. Changes in survival rates suggest that future older adults will:

    a. be more likely to live in 4-5 generational households
    X b. be more likely to be members of 4-5 generational families
    c. be more likely to have children and grandchildren caring for them
    d. have many members of step-families to care for them

4. Changes in the fertility rates have resulted in a situation today in which:

    a. more adult children are available as caregivers for the aged
    X b. women can expect to spend more years caring for a parent than a child
    c. women can expect to spend more years caring for children than for older relatives
    d. fewer people will have grandparents surviving to old age

5. First time grandparenthood today generally occurs:

    a. at an earlier age
    b. at a later age
    X c. at a wide variety of ages from 35 to 75
    d. more often with step-grandchildren than with natural grandchildren

6. Differences in male and female longevity, as well as differences in attitudes about social networks, will result in:

X a. more men relying on intragenerational ties
   b. more women turning to their sons for support
   c. more women living with their husbands in old age
   d. more men outliving their wives

7. Despite increasing life expectancy, married couples today are no more likely to reach their golden wedding anniversary than in the past because:

X a. Divorce rates have increased.
   b. Death rates among the old-old have not declined.
   c. Marriage takes place much later today than in the past.
   d. Life expectancy for older men has not improved.

8. The increased number of women in the workforce has resulted in the following changes in family caregiving responsibilities and services:

   a. more men assuming caregiving roles
X b. greater demands on women to provide caregiving in addition to theiremployment
   c. increased support from the federal government for parental care
   d. all of the above
   e. none of the above

9. Future cohorts of older persons will experience:

   a. more opportunities for job retraining
   b. increased alternatives to full-time work after retiring
   c. a greater proportion of their lives in retirement
X d. all of the above
   e. none of the above

10. Changes in attitudes toward employment and retirement today will result in:

   a. more people staying in their first jobs longer
X b. increased numbers of adults seeking second and third careers
   c. increased demands for technical education in high school
   d. more people completing college by the age of 22

11. Future cohorts of older people will view leisure as:

   a. a reward for many years of work
   b. difficult to achieve because of demands for lifelong employment

X c. a continuation of their lifestyles during their working years
   d. something to avoid because it is contrary to the work ethic

12. The growth in computer technology suggests that future cohorts of older people will:

X a. have the capability to be linked to the outside world even if they cannot leave their homes
   b. be left behind in electronic communication because they are unfamiliar with computers
   c. survive on their own with no input from their families
   d. spend more for their home maintenance

13. Baby boomers who become "senior boomers" will differ from earlier cohorts of older people in which of the following ways?

   a. They will be healthier and more oriented toward health promotion.
   b. They will generally be financially better off.
   c. They will be culturally and racially more diverse.
   d. none of the above
X e. all of the above

14. Health care for older cohorts in the future will be characterized by which of the following:

   a. less use of ambulatory services and more hospital days of care
   b. greater competition for older patients
X c. managed are and an emphasis on cost containment
   d. all of the above
   e. none of the above

15. The increase of the older population has raised numerous ethical issues because:

   a. medical technology has made it possible to extended a healthy life, followed by a quick illness and death
   b. the timing, place and conditions of death are increasingly under medical control.
X c. agreement does not exist about whether, how and under what circumstances to prolong life
   d. medical technology has made it easier to draw a clear line between living and dying

True or False

1. Future cohorts of older adults will be more likely than previous cohorts to view public assistance as a right.

   True __X__   False _____

2. Future adults will be more likely to experience cyclical shifts between education, careers, and caregiving across the life span.

   True __X__   False _____

3. By the year 2000, women and people of color will account for the majority of the labor force.

   True __X__   False _____

4. There is a growing trend for older people who spent their earlier years in suburbs to move to city centers.

   True _____   False __X__

5. The growth in home-based services and computers suggests that more of the future older population can remain in their own homes.

   True __X__   False _____

6. Reverse mortgage plans have resulted in more older people losing their homes to banks as they outlive their mortgages.

   True _____   False __X__

7. The growth of special hospital programs for older people has also benefited the uninsured older cohort.

   True _____   False __X__

8. Ethical questions are increasing about the health care of older people largely because of diminishing resources and the increased costs of such care.

   True __X__   False _____

9. The increased number of training opportunities in geriatric health will probably result in higher health care costs for older people.

   True _____   False _X_

10. By the year 2000, the single most important feature of the older population will be its racial diversity.

    True _____   False _X_

11. The verticalized or "beanpole" family structure refers to the fact that fewer family members are available within each generation to provide assistance to each other.

    True _X_   False _____

12. Fortunately, most corporations have now instituted programs to assist family members caring for older relatives.

    True _____   False _X_

13. Successful aging is equated with productive and work-oriented roles in our society.

    True _____   False _X_

14. The growth of medical technology has added to the problem of rationing health care.

    True _X_   False _____

15. When a physician defines a situation as medically futile, this means that treatment offers no therapeutic benefit to a patient.

    True _X_   False _____

RESOURCE DIRECTORY

NATIONAL ORGANIZATIONS AND AGENCIES RELATED TO AGING

ACTION - Older Americans Volunteer Programs, 1100 Vermont Ave. NW, Washington, DC 20525, (202) 634-9108.

> The federal agency which coordinates volunteer programs such as RSVP, FGP, and Green Thumb, SCORE, ACE, VISTA, Peace Corps, and Senior Companion.

Administration on Aging (AoA), Department of Health and Human Services, 330 Independence Avenue SW, Room 4146, Washington, DC 20201, (202) 245-2158.

> The federal agency responsible for administering grant programs to the states. It is also a central source of information, technical assistance, and evaluation in the area of aging programs.

Alliance for Aging Research, 2021 K Street NW, Suite 710, Washington, DC 20006, (202) 293-2856.

Alzheimer's Disease and Related Disorders Association Inc. (ADRDA), 919 N. Michigan Ave., Suite 1000, Chicago, IL 60611-1676 (312) 335-8700.

> Publishes Alzheimer's Disease and Related Disorders Newsletter, useful to both families and professionals. Provides research updates and news of Alzheimer's Support Information Service Team chapters from around the country. Information packet available for $6.

Alzheimer's Disease Education and Referral Center (ADEAR), P.O. Box 8250, Silver Spring, MD 20907, (301) 495-3311.

> Established by the National Institute on Aging, ADEAR distributes information to health professionals, patients and their families, and the general public on Alzheimer's disease, current research activities, and available services. Publishes an Alzheimer's disease information packet.

American Association of Homes for the Aging (AAHA), 901 E. Street NW, Suite 500, Washington, DC, 20044, (202) 783-2243.

American Association of Retired Persons (AARP), 601 E Street NW, Washington, DC, 20049, (202) 434-2300.

> AARP offers a wide range of publications and services for persons over 55, including a monthly publication for all members, Modern Maturity. AARP has a newer division called AIM (Action for Independent Maturity) for persons aged 50-65, as well as the Institute of Lifetime Learning:
> 215 Long Beach Blvd., Long Beach, CA 90802.

American Federation for Aging Research, 725 Park Ave, New York, NY 10021, (212) 570-2090.

> This organization encourages and supports basic and clinical research in biomedical aspects of aging.

American Foundation for the Blind, 1615 M Street NW, Suite 205, Washington, DC 20036, (202) 457-1487.

> A national clearinghouse for information about blindness and visual impairment. Updated list and designation of nationwide low-vision centers; series of self-help manuals; catalogs of low-vision aids, including clocks, watches, timers, games, medical aids, sewing and writing aids, tools, and measuring devices. Publishes Aids and Appliances for the Blind and Visually Impaired.

American Geriatrics Society Inc., 770 Lexington Ave., Suite 300, New York, NY 10021, (212) 543-7446.

> This organization emphasizes research and publication in the medical aspects of aging, and publishes the Journal of the American Geriatrics Society.

American Health Care Association, 1201 L Street NW, Washington, DC 20005, (202) 842-8444.

> A federation of state associations of nursing homes. Publishes information on characteristics and status of profit and nonprofit homes.

American Printing House for the Blind, P.O. Box 6085, Avenue, Louisville, KY 40206, (800) 223-1839.

> Offers a catalog of writing aids, tape recorders, and educational materials, as well as A Catalog of Large Type Print.

American Society for Geriatric Dentistry, 211 East Chicago Ave., Chicago, IL 60611, (312) 440-2661.

> The ASGD offers membership to dental professionals interested in clinical and research issues concerning the elderly. A monthly newsletter is published on relevant geriatric dental issues.

American Society on Aging, 833 Market Street, Suite 511 San Francisco, CA 94103, (415) 974-9600.

> National organization of educators, practitioners, and elderly. Holds national and regional conferences. Publishes bimonthly newspaper, "The Aging Connection", and journal Generations.

American Speech-Language Hearing Association, 10801 Rockville Pike, Dept. AP, Rockville, MD 20852, (301) 897-5700.

> Can answer questions or mail information on hearing aids or hearing loss and communication problems in older people. Can also provide list of certified audiologists in each state.

Arthritis Foundation, P.O. Box 19000, Atlanta, GA 30326, (404)872-7100 or (800)283-7800.

> The foundation conducts research into the prevention and treatment of arthritis and provides services and education. They publish many helpful pamphlets, including The Self-Help Manual for Patients With Arthritis, which lists equipment and devices.

Association for Gerontology in Higher Education (AGHE), 1001 Connecticut Ave. NW, Suite 410, Washington, DC 20036-5504. (202) 429-9277.

> An organization of 300 colleges and universities involved in aging through education, research, and public service. Publishes National Directory of Educational Programs in Gerontology.

Better Hearing Institute, Box 1840, Washington, DC 20013, (703) 642-0850.

> Maintains a toll-free Hearing Helpline that provides information about hearing aids, tinnitus, nerve deafness, special devices, and other problems related to hearing loss.

Choice in Dying, 200 Varick Street, New York, NY 10014, (212) 366-5540 or (800) 989-WILL.

> Formerly Concern for Dying and the Society for the Right to Die. Provides statutory advance directives for each state, free of charge, and other materials and services relating to end-of-life medical care.

Citizens for the Improvement of Nursing Homes (CINH). 3530 Stone Way North, Seattle, WA 98103, (206) 461-4553.

Elder Care Locator, (800) 677-1116.

> This national toll-free number is designed to help identify community resources for seniors anywhere in the United States. The name, address, and zip code of the person needing assistance allows the Elder Care Locator to identify the nearest information and assistance sources in that person's community. Call between 9:00 a.m. and 8:00 p.m. Eastern Time.

Elderhostel, 80 Boylston Street, Suite 400, Boston, MA 02116, (617) 426-8056.

> Offers educational opportunities through colleges nationwide and abroad.

Families USA, 1334 G Street NW, Washington, DC 20005, (202) 737-6340.

Federal Council on Aging, Room 4243 HHS North Building, 330 Independence Avenue SW, Washington, DC 20201. (202) 245-2451.

Foundation for Grandparenting, P.O. Box 326, Cohasset, MA 02025.

> A national organization that offers advice and assistance on grandparents' visitation rights, and on grandparent/grandchildren programs nationally and internationally.

Gatekeeper Program, Spokane Community Mental Health Center Elderly Services, South 107 Division, Spokane, WA 99202, (509) 838-4651.

> This program utilizes non-traditional referral sources who come into contact with high-risk elderly individuals. They offer a training video, training manual, and other material relative to the concept of active case finding and in-home delivery systems.

Gerontological Society of America. 1275 K Street, NW, Suite 350, Washington, DC 20005-4006, (202) 842-1275.

A professional organization devoted to the research, publication, and exchange of information on aging. The society sponsors an annual conference, and publishes a newletter and bimonthly research journals, Journals of Gerontology and The Gerontologist.

Gray Panthers, 2025 Pennsylvania Ave. NW, Suite 821, Washington, DC, 20006, (202) 466-3132.

National intergenerational activist movement concerned with eradication of "ageism"--discrimination based on age. The Panthers hold conferences and workshops, maintain a speakers' bureau, and help groups organize.

Help for Incontinent People (HIP), P.O. Box 544, Union, SC 29379, (800) 252-3337 or (803) 579-7900.

This is a self-help and patient advocacy group that offers encouragement, information, and resources listings for incontinent people. It also publishes a quarterly newsletter that provides practical advice, as well as the following helpful pamphlets: "Bladder Retraining" and "Resource Guide of Continence Products and Services."

Hemlock Society, P.O. Box 11830, Eugene, OR 97440, (503) 342-5748.

International Federation on Ageing, 601 E. Street, NW, Washington, DC 20049

A private nonprofit organization linking approximately 100 associations that represent or serve older persons at the grassroots level in 50 nations around the world.

Library of Congress, Blind and Physically Handicapped Division, 1291 Taylor Street NW, Washington, DC 20542, (202) 707-5104.

Resource for talking books for the visually impaired.

National Action Forum for Midlife and Older Women, Box 816, Stony Brook, NY 11790.

Publishes Hotflash: A Newsletter for Midlife and Older Women, that covers a wide range of topics of interest to middle-aged and older women.

National Association of Area Agencies on Aging, 1112 16th Street NW, Suite 100, Washington, DC 20036, (202) 296-8130.

National Asian Pacific Center on Aging, 1511 Third Ave., Suite 914, Melbourne Tower, Seattle, WA 98101, (206) 624-1221.

Sponsors employment programs and develops strategies to increase accessibility of federal programs for low-income Asian-Pacific elders.

National Association for Hispanic Elderly, 3325 Wilshire Blvd., Suite 800, Los Angeles, CA 90010, (213) 487-1922.

Provides social services and employment programs for low-income Hispanic elderly. Offers information and referral for SSI eligibility. Produces documentaries and public service announcements.

National Association for Home Care (NAHC), 519 C Street, NE, Stanton Park, Washington, DC 20002, (202) 547-7424.

NAHC monitors federal and state activities affecting home care and focuses on issues relating to home health care. They publish Caring Magazine on a bimonthly basis.

National Association of Nutrition and Aging Services Programs, 2675 44th Street, SW, Suite 305, Grand Rapids, MI 49509, (616) 531-8700.

National Association of Retired Federal Employees, 1533 New Hampshire Avenue NW, Washington, DC 20036, (202) 234-0832.

National organization which represents the interests of retired federal employees. Publishes a monthly magazine and offers special life, health, and auto insurance rates.

National Caucus and Center on Black Aged, 1424 K Street N.W., Suite 500, Washington, DC 20005, (202) 637-8400.

An advocate organization working on behalf of older black persons. Publishes a newsletter, conducts research, and disseminates information on aging and aged African Americans.

National Center for Voluntary Action, Volunteer--the National Center, 1111 N. 19th Street, Suite 500, Arlington, VA 22209, (703) 276-0542.

A private nonprofit organization concerned with promoting volunteerism nationally. It helps communities start voluntary action centers and maintains a central data bank on volunteerism.

National Citizens' Coalition for Nursing Home Reform, 1224 M Street, NW, Suite 301, Washington, DC, 20005, (202) 393-2018.

> The coalition is comprised of groups and individuals committed to improving the quality of life and care for nursing home residents. They serve as a voice enabling consumers to be heard. They publish a journal, Collation, for advocates working on nursing home issues.

National Clearinghouse on Aging, Administration on Aging, OHD/DHHS, 330 Independence Avenue, SW, Washington, DC 20201, (202) 245-0350.

> Federal office responsible for collecting, analyzing, and disseminating information about aging and aging programs. Serves as a national clearinghouse for such information.

National Coalition of Grandparents(NCOG), 137 Larkin, Madison, WI 53705, (608) 238-8751.

> Works toward legislative changes to ensure a child's right to a safe, stable environment and to strengthen intergenerational family bonds.

National Committee to Preserve Social Security and Medicare, 2000 K Street, Washington, DC 20006, (202) 822-9459.

> Publishes Viewpoint, an analysis of current legislation and the committee's recommended action.

National Council of Senior Citizens(NCSC), 1331 F Street N.W., Washington, D.C. 20004-1171, (202) 347-8800.

> NCSC is composed of representatives of seniors' organizations throughout the nation. Its foci are on education and social action.

National Council on the Aging Inc. (NCOA), 409 Third St.,SW, Second Floor, Washington, DC 20024, (202) 479-1200.

> A private, nonprofit corporation which serves as a central resource for information, technical assistance, training, planning and consultation in gerontology.

National Council of Senior Citizens, 1331 F Street NW, Washington, DC 20004-1171, (202) 347-8800.

National Hearing Aid Helpline, (800) 521-5247.

Provides information on hearing aids and distributes a directory of hearing aid specialists certified by the National Hearing Aid Society.

National Indian Council on Aging, City Center, Suite 510 West, Albuquerque, NM 87110, (505) 888-3302.

Purpose is to improve the lives of Indian and Alaskan Native elders through specialized activities. They maintain a cooperative relationship with a number of federal agencies, conducting research on aging and issuing reports on the needs of Indian and Alaskan Native elders.

National Institute on Adult Day Care, 600 Maryland Avenue SW, West Wing 100, Washington, DC 20024, (800) 424-9046.

Publishes a directory of adult day care in the United States. Ask for order #2022.

National Institute on Aging (NIA), Building 31, Room 5C35, Bethesda, MD 20892, (301) 496-1752.

Prints fact sheets on various aspects of aging.

National Institute of Neurological Disorders and Stroke, P.O. Box 5801, Bethesda, MD 20824, (301) 496-5751.

This institute offers information and publications on disorders such as dementia, stroke, brain tumors, and Parkinson's disease.

National Osteoporosis Foundation, 1150 17th Street NW, Suite 500, Washington, DC 20036, (202) 223-2226.

National Resource Center on Health Promotion and Aging, 601 E Street NW, Suite B5, Washington, DC 20049.

Publishes a bimonthly newsletter, "Perspectives in Health Promotion and Aging," containing updates on health issues of interest to caregivers.

National Shared Housing Resource Center, 431 Pine Street, Burlington, VT 05401, (802) 862-2727.

The center publishes a pamphlet, Is Homesharing for You? A Self-Help Guide for Homeowners and Renters. They also serve as a resource center and offer technical assistance for 350 shared housing projects nationally.

National Self-Help Clearinghouse, 33 West 42nd St., Room 620N , New York, NY 10036, (212) 840-1259.

> Publishes a bimonthly newsletter, The Self-Help Reporter, and keeps a record of self-help clearinghouses throughout the country.

National Senior Citizens' Law Center, 1815 H Street NW, Suite 700, Washington, DC 20006, (202) 887-5280.

> A central national resource for legal services programs serving low income elders; works at federal, state, and local levels to see that needs of low income older adults are met.

Older Women's League, 666 Eleventh Street NW, Suite 700, Washington, DC 20001, (202)783-6686.

> National advocacy and educational organization. Focus on issues of economics, security, health and long-term care, and caregiving.

Parent Care. Gerontology Center, 4089 Dole, Human Development Center, University of Kansas, Lawrence, KS 66045, (913) 864-4130.

Raising Our Children's Kids: An Intergenerational Network of Grandparenting, Inc. (ROCKING), P.O. Box 96, Niles, MI 49120, (616) 683-9038.

> Maintains a directory of support groups for caregivers by each state. Now seeking the passage of a mandated kinship care program in all 50 states.

SAGE: Senior Action in a Gay Environment, 208 West 13th Street, New York, NY 10011, (212) 441-2247.

> Newsletter and resource directory about groups providing services to older gay men and lesbians.

Self-Help for Hard of Hearing People (SHHH), 7800 Wisconsin Ave., Bethesda, MD 20892, (301) 657-2248 or TTY (301) 657-2299.

> SHHH is a national self-help organization for those who are hard of hearing. Publishes a bimonthly journal reporting the experiences of those with hearing impairments as well as new developments in the field of hearing loss.

U.S. Department of Commerce--Social and Economics Statistics Administration, Bureau of the Census, Washington DC 20233, (301) 763-5190.

This agency publishes the Current Population Reports which include population, income, education, housing, etc. data.

JOURNALS AND MAGAZINES

Aging. Published by Administration on Aging, Washington, DC 20201. Available from superintendent of Documents from U.S. Government Printing Office, Washington, DC 20204-9731, $15.

Good general coverage of what is happening in aging throughout the country. Includes information on programs, legislation, state and federal agencies, gerontological publications, and conferences.

Aging and Society. Cambridge University Press, 40 West 20 St., New York, NY 10022, (212) 924-3900.

American Journal of Alzheimer's Care and Related Disorders and Research. 470 Boston Post Road, Weston, MA 02193.

Clinical Gerontologist: The Journal of Aging and Mental Health. The Haworth Press, Inc., 12 West 32nd Street, New York, NY 10001.

Dynamic Years. American Association of Retired Persons (AARP), 215 Long Beach Blvd., Long Beach, CA 90801. Bimonthly, $7/year.

Covers topics on preretirement planning, specifically for persons age 50-64.

Generations. 833 Market Street, Suite 516, San Francisco, CA 94103. Published by the American Society on Aging, Journal of Western Gerontological Society.

Oriented to practitioners.

Geriatrics. Edgell Communications 7500 Old Oak Blvd., Cleveland, OH 44130.

A medical journal which covers recent developments and findings in geriatrics. Also includes book reviews, abstracts, and information on recent legislation.

International Journal of Aging and Human Development. Baywood Publishing Co., Inc., 120 Marine St., Box D, Farmingdale, NY 11735.

Journal of Gerontological Social Work. The Haworth Press, 12 West 32nd St., New York, NY 10001.

AARP Highlights. Published by AARP, 1909 K Street N.W., Washington, DC 20049.

> Covers local AARP activities, national developments, general interest articles.

Collation. National Citizens' Coalition for NH Reform, 1424 16th St. NW, Washington, DC 20036, (202)-797-0657.

> A journal for advocates working on nursing home issues. Includes legislative updates, organizational strategies, and litigation experiences. National Citizens' Coalition for Nursing Home Reform is a coalition of groups and individuals committed to improving the quality of life and care for nursing home residents.

Elder Press. The Elvirita Lewis Foundation, Suite 144, Airport Park Plaza, 255 N. El Cielo Road, Palm Springs, CA 92262, (619) 397-4552.

The Senior Citizen News. Published by the National Council of Senior Citizens Inc., 925 15th Street N.W., Washington, DC 20005.

> Provides information on national legislation and happenings of concern to the elderly.

RELATED PUBLICATIONS

Resources for the Aging: An Action Handbook. Published by NCOA, 600 Maryland Avenue S.W., West Wing 100, Washington, DC 20024 (202) 479-1200. Prepared for OEO, second edition .

> Designed to guide communities and individuals in their efforts at helping the aged poor. Techniques of utilizing federal programs, voluntary agencies, foundations, and trusts are covered.